SONGS OF NATURE

JOHN BURROUGHS

SONGS
OF NATURE

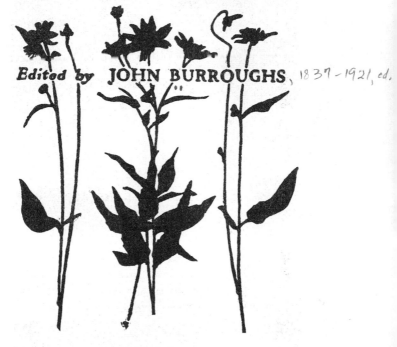

Edited by JOHN BURROUGHS, 1837-1921, ed.

Granger Index Reprint Series

BOOKS FOR LIBRARIES PRESS
FREEPORT, NEW YORK

PN
6110
.N2
B8
1969

First Published 1901
Reprinted 1969

STANDARD BOOK NUMBER:
8369-6070-x

LIBRARY OF CONGRESS CATALOG CARD NUMBER:
79-98077

INTRODUCTION

By John Burroughs

N compiling this anthology of Nature poetry I have been guided entirely by my own taste in such matters; I have here gathered together such poems as I myself prefer amid the material at my disposal. This is according to the wishes of the publishers, who desired that the collection should be mine in a real sense, and thus carry with it such savor of originality as one man's preferences may give to such a work. I trust I have not carried my personal likings too far, or to the point of giving expression to any mere eccentricities of taste in my selections. To make the work individual and yet of a high average of excellence has been my hope.

In such matters it all comes back after all to one's likes or dislikes. One may think he is trying the poem by the standard of the best that has been done in this line while he is only trying it by his own conception of that standard. So much of that standard as is vital in his own mind, he can apply and no more. His own individual taste and judgment, clarified and disciplined, of course, by wide reading and reflection, are his *only guides. The standard of the best is not something that any man can apply, as he can the standard of weights and measures; only the best can apply the best.*

This collection represents on the whole my judgment of the best Nature poems at my disposal in the language. I am surprised at the amount of so-called Nature poetry that has been added to English literature during the past fifty years, but I find only a little of it of permanent worth. The painted, padded, and perfumed Nature of so many of the younger poets I cannot stand at all. I have not knowingly admitted any poem that was not true to my own observations of Nature — or that diverged at all from the facts of the case. Thus, a poem that shows the swallow perched upon the barn in October I could not accept, because the swallow leaves us in August; or a poem that makes the chestnut bloom with the lilac — an instance I came across in my reading — would be ruled out on like grounds; or when I find poppies blooming in the corn in an American poem, as I several times have done, I pass by on the other side.

In a bird poem I want the real bird as a basis — not merely a description of it, but its true place in the season and in the landscape, and no liberties taken with the facts of its life history. I must see or hear or feel the live bird in the

verses, as one does in *Wordsworth's* "*Cuckoo*,"
or *Emerson's* "*Titmouse*" or *Trowbridge's* "*Pe-
wee*." *Lowell* is not quite true to the facts when
in one of his poems he makes the male oriole as-
sist at nest building. The male may seem to
superintend the work, but he does not actually
lend a hand. Give me the real bird first, and
then all the poetry that can be evoked from it.

I am aware that there is another class of bird
poems, or poems inspired by birds, such as
Keats's "*Ode to a Nightingale*," in which there is
little or no natural history, not even of the subli-
mated kind, and yet that take high rank as
poems. It is the "waking dream" in these po-
ems, the translation of sensuous impressions into
spiritual longings and attractions that is the
secret of their power. When the poet can give
us himself, we can well afford to miss the bird.

The fanciful and allegorical treatment of Nat-
ure is for the most part distasteful to me. I do
not want a mere rhymed description of an object
or scene, nor a fanciful dressing of it up in po-
etic imagery. I want it mirrored in the heart
and life of the poet; true to the reality without
and to the emotion within. The one thing that
makes a poem anyway is emotion — the emotion of
love, of beauty, of sublimity — and these emotions
playing about the reality result in the true Nat-
ure poetry as in *Wordsworth, Emerson,* and

Bryant. The poet is not so much to paint Nature as he is to recreate her. He interprets her when he infuses his own love into her.

I have also avoided all poems in which the form was difficult. The form of the masters like Tennyson and Wordsworth is easy, easy as it is in organic Nature in her happy moods. I do not want to be compelled to expend any force upon the poet's form — I want it all for his thought. A tortuous and difficult channel may add to the beauty of a mountain brook, but it does not add to the beauty of a poem. The mountain-brook quality must be in the spirit, the conception. I have always been shy of the sonnet, because it so rarely flows; it is labored; it is arbitrary, with sentences cut in the middle and gasping out a feeble rhyme. But the sonnets of at least one of our younger poets — author of " The Fields of Dawn" — actually flow, and one can read them without any mental contortion, as of course he can the great sonnets of Shakespeare and Milton and Wordsworth.

One of our young Southern poets has written many Nature poems that are based on real love and observation, and that abound in striking and beautiful lines, but his form is involved and difficult, and I have not been able to find in his numerous volumes one whole poem that I could take.

The standard New England poets are not more largely represented in my collection, because *of copyright restrictions. A few of our minor poets are also absent for the same reason.*

I am indebted to Houghton, Mifflin & Company for special permission to use such poems as I have selected from the works of Longfellow, Emerson, Lowell, Whittier, Holmes, Bret Harte, Frank Bolles, Aldrich, Celia Thaxter, Thoreau, Miss Thomas, Trowbridge, Edgar Fawcett, Maurice Thompson, Samuel Longfellow, Helen Gray Cone, E. C. Stedman, Frank D. Sherman, Mary Clemmer Ames, Anna Boynton Averill, Dinah Maria Mulock Craik, Wilson Flagg, William Dean Howells, Charles Kingsley, Lucy Larcom, George Parsons Lathrop, Lloyd Mifflin, James Montgomery, Nora Perry, Charles G. D. Roberts, Henry Timrod, Jones Very, and A. West.

I am also indebted to D. Appleton & Company for five of the poems of Bryant; to the Century Company for four poems from Richard Watson Gilder's "Five Books of Song," and two poems by Robert Underwood Johnson; to Robert Clark Company for poems by William D. Gallagher; to Henry Holt & Company for the poem by Robert Kelley Weeks; to Lee & Shepard for the poem by David Atwood Wasson; to J. B. Lippincott Company for Harrison Smith Morris's poem "The Lonely Bird" from "Madonna and other Poems," and for the selection entitled "The Closing Scene" from Thomas Buchanan Read's Poems; to Longmans, Green & Company for the poem by *Andrew Lang*, and Poems by *Sarah Piatt*; to *David McKay* for seven poems from *Walt Whitman's* "*Leaves of Grass*"; to *Small, Maynard & Company* for two selections from *Bliss Carman's* "*Songs from Vagabondia*," and two from "*Poems, by John B. Tabb*"; to *A. M. Robertson* for the poem by *Charles Keeler*; to *J. H. Russell* for poems by *Robert Burns Wilson*.

My thanks are further due to *Miss Cornelia Holroyd Bradley* for permission to use the poem by her mother, *Mrs. Mary Emily Bradley*; to *Rollin H. Cooke* for permission to reprint the poem by *Rose Terry Cooke*; to *Charlton H. Royal*, executor of the estate of *Thomas MacKellar*, for allowing the reprint of "*The Troublesome Fly*"; to *Mrs. Florence Laighton* for permission to use the poem by *Albert Laighton*; to *Annabel Irvine Brown* for permission to use the poems of her father, *J. P. Irvine*, and to the following authors for the use of their poems: *Henry Abbey, Mrs. Elizabeth Akers Allen, Joel Benton, Myron B. Benton, Mrs. Darmesteter, Charles DeKay, Mary Isabella Forsyth, Hamlin Garland, Harriet McEwen Kimball, George Murray, Mrs. Sara L. Oberholtzer, Charles Warren Stoddard*, and *Mrs. Nelly Hart Woodworth*.

JOHN BURROUGHS.

September, 1901.

SONGS OF NATURE

THE RETIREMENT

By Charles Cotton

AREWELL, thou busy world, and may
    We never meet again ;
Here I can eat and sleep and pray,
And do more good in one short day
    Than he who his whole age outwears
Upon the most conspicuous theatres,
Where naught but vanity and vice appears.

Good God ! how sweet are all things here !
How beautiful the fields appear !
    How cleanly do we feed and lie !
Lord ! what good hours do we keep !
How quietly we sleep !
    What peace, what unanimity !
How innocent from the lewd fashion
Is all our business, all our recreation !

O, how happy here's our leisure !
O, how innocent our pleasure !
O ye valleys !   O ye mountains !
O ye groves, and crystal fountains !
How I love, at liberty,
By turns to come and visit ye !

I

Dear solitude, the soul's best friend,
That man acquainted with himself dost make,
And all his Maker's wonders to intend,
    With thee I here converse at will,
    And would be glad to do so still,
For it is thou alone that keep'st the soul
    awake.

How calm and quiet a delight
    Is it, alone,
To read and meditate and write,
    By none offended, and offending none !
To walk, ride, sit, or sleep at one's own ease ;
And, pleasing a man's self, none other to dis-
    please.

O my beloved nymph, fair Dove,
Princess of rivers, how I love
    Upon thy flowery banks to lie,
And view thy silver stream,
When gilded by a Summer's beam !
    And in it all thy wanton fry
    Playing at liberty,
And, with my angle, upon them
    The all of treachery
    I ever learned industriously to try !

Such streams Rome's yellow Tiber cannot show,
The Iberian Tagus, or Ligurian Po ;
The Maese, the Danube, and the Rhine,
Are puddle-water, all, compared with thine ;
And Loire's pure streams yet too polluted are
With thine, much purer, to compare ;

The rapid Garonne and the winding Seine
Are both too mean,
    Beloved Dove, with thee
    To vie priority;
Nay, Tame and Isis, when conjoined, submit,
And lay their trophies at thy silver feet.

O my beloved rocks, that rise
To awe the earth and brave the skies!
From some aspiring mountain's crown
    How dearly do I love,
Giddy with pleasure to look down;
    And from the vales to view the noble heights
        above;
O my beloved caves! from dog-star's heat,
And all anxieties, my safe retreat;
What safety, privacy, what true delight,
In the artificial light
    Your gloomy entrails make,
    Have I taken, do I take!
How oft, when grief has made me fly,
To hide me from society
E'en of my dearest friends, have I,
    In your recesses' friendly shade,
    All my sorrows open laid,
And my most secret woes intrusted to your privacy!

Lord! would men let me alone,
What an over-happy one
    Should I think myself to be—
Might I in this desert place,
(Which most men in discourse disgrace)
    Live but undisturbed and free!

Here in this despised recess,
    Would I, maugre Winter's cold,
And the Summer's worst excess,
    Try to live out to sixty full years old ;
And, all the while,
    Without an envious eye
On any thriving under Fortune's smile,
    Contented live, and then contented die.

FOR ONE RETIRED INTO THE COUNTRY

By Charles Wesley

ENCE, lying world, with all thy
    care,
    With all thy shows of good and
    fair,
        Of beautiful or great !
    Stand with thy slighted charms
    aloof,
Nor dare invade my peaceful roof,
    Or trouble my retreat.

Far from thy mad fantastic ways
I here have found a resting-place
    Of poor wayfaring men :
Calm as the hermit in his grot
I here enjoy my happy lot,
    And solid pleasures gain.

Along the hill or dewy mead
In sweet forgetfulness I tread,
        Or wander through the grove;
As Adam in his native seat,
In all his works my God I meet,
        The object of my love.

I see his beauty in the flower:
To shade my walks and deck my bower
        His love and wisdom join;
Him in the feathered choir I hear,
And own, while all my soul is ear,
        The music is divine.

In yon unbounded plain I see
A sketch of his immensity
        Who spans these ample skies;
Whose presence makes the happy place,
And opens in the wilderness
        A blooming paradise.

Oh, would he now himself impart,
And fix the Eden in my heart,
        The sense of sin forgiven:
How should I then throw off my load,
And walk delightfully with God,
        And follow Christ to heaven!

ODE ON SOLITUDE

By *Alexander Pope*

APPY the man whose wish and
    care
   A few paternal acres bound,
Content to breathe his native air
   In his own ground:

Whose herds with milk, whose
    fields with bread,
  Whose flocks supply him with attire;
Whose trees in summer yield him shade,
   In winter fire:

Blest, who can unconcern'dly find
   Hours, days, and years slide soft away;
In health of body, peace of mind,
   Quiet by day:

Sound sleep by night, study and ease,
   Together mixt, sweet recreation;
And innocence, which most does please,
   With meditation.

Thus let me live, unseen, unknown;
   Thus, unlamented, let me die,
Steal from the world, and not a stone
   Tell where I lie.

HYMN TO CYNTHIA

By Ben Jonson

QUEEN and Huntress, chaste and
    fair,
  Now the sun is laid to sleep,
Seated in thy silver chair,
  State in wonted manner keep:
    Hesperus entreats thy light,
    Goddess excellently bright!

Earth, let not thy envious shade
  Dare itself to interpose;
Cynthia's shining orb was made
  Heaven to clear when day did close;
    Bless us then with wishéd sight,
    Goddess excellently bright!

Lay thy bow of pearl apart
  And thy crystal-shining quiver;
Give unto the flying hart
  Space to breathe, how short soever;
    Thou that mak'st a day of night,
    Goddess excellently bright!

RETIREMENT

By *Thomas Warton*

INSCRIPTION IN A HERMITAGE

ENEATH this stony roof re-
  clined,
I soothe to peace my pensive
  mind ;
And while, to shade my lowly
  cave,
Embowering elms their umbrage
  wave ;
And while the maple dish is mine —
The beechen cup, unstained with wine —
I scorn the gay licentious crowd,
Nor heed the toys that deck the proud.

Within my limits, lone and still,
The blackbird pipes in artless trill ;
Fast by my couch, congenial guest,
The wren has wove her mossy nest ;
From busy scenes and brighter skies,
To lurk with innocence, she flies,
Here hopes in safe repose to dwell,
Nor aught suspects the sylvan cell.

At morn I take my customed round,
To mark how buds yon shrubby mound,
And every opening primrose count,
That trimly paints my blooming mount ;

Or o'er the sculptures, quaint and rude,
That grace my gloomy solitude,
I teach in winding wreaths to stray
Fantastic ivy's gadding spray.

At eve, within yon studious nook,
I ope my brass-embossed book,
Portrayed with many a holy deed
Of martyrs, crowned with heavenly meed;
Then, as my taper waxes dim,
Chant, ere I sleep, my measured hymn,
And at the close, the gleams behold
Of parting wings, be-dropt with gold.

While such pure joys my bliss create,
Who but would smile at guilty state?
Who but would wish his holy lot
In calm oblivion's humble grot?
Who but would cast his pomp away,
To take my staff, and amice gray;
And to the world's tumultuous stage
Prefer the blameless hermitage?

PACK CLOUDS AWAY

By *Thomas Heywood*

ACK clouds away, and welcome
    day,
    With night we banish sor-
      row;
    Sweet air, blow soft; mount,
      lark, aloft,
    To give my love good-morrow.
Wings from the wind to please her mind,
    Notes from the lark I'll borrow:
Bird, prune thy wing; nightingale, sing,
    To give my love good-morrow.
    To give my love good-morrow,
    Notes from them all I'll borrow.

Wake from thy nest, robin redbreast,
    Sing, birds, in every furrow;
And from each hill let music shrill
    Give my fair love good-morrow.
Blackbird and thrush in every bush,
    Stare, linnet, and cock-sparrow,
You petty elves, amongst yourselves,
    Sing my fair love good-morrow.
    To give my love good-morrow,
    Sing, birds, in every furrow.

TO BLOSSOMS

By Robert Herrick

FAIR pledges of a fruitful tree,
    Why do ye fall so fast?
    Your date is not so past,
But you may stay yet here a
    while
To blush and gently smile,
    And go at last.

What! were ye born to be
    An hour or half's delight,
    And so to bid good-night?
'Twas pity Nature brought ye forth,
Merely to show your worth,
    And lose you quite.

THE HOUSEKEEPER

By Charles Lamb

THE frugal snail, with forecast of repose,
    Carries his house with him where'er he goes;
    Peeps out, — and if there comes a shower
        of rain,
Retreats to his small domicile again.
Touch but a tip of him, a horn, — 'tis well, —
He curls up in his sanctuary shell.
He's his own landlord, his own tenant; stay
Long as he will, he dreads no Quarter Day.
Himself he boards and lodges; both invites
And feasts himself; sleeps with himself o' nights.

He spares the upholsterer trouble to procure
Chattels ; himself is his own furniture,
And his sole riches.   Whereso'er he roam, —
Knock when you will, — he's sure to be at home.

THE CLOUD

By *Percy Bysshe Shelley*

BRING fresh showers for the
    thirsting flowers,
    From the seas and the streams ;
I bear light shade for the leaves
    when laid
    In their noonday dreams.
From my wings are shaken the
    dews that waken
  The sweet buds every one,
When rocked to rest on their mother's breast,
    As she dances about the sun.
I wield the flail of the lashing hail,
    And whiten the green plains under ;
And then again I dissolve it in rain,
    And laugh as I pass in thunder.

I sift the snow on the mountains below,
    And their great pines groan aghast ;
And all the night 'tis my pillow white,
    While I sleep in the arms of the blast.
Sublime on the towers of my skyey bowers,
    Lightning my pilot sits ;
In a cavern under is fettered the thunder,
    It struggles and howls at fits ;

Over earth and ocean, with gentle motion,
　　This pilot is guiding me,
Lured by the love of the genii that move
　　In the depths of the purple sea;
Over the rills, and the crags, and the hills,
　　Over the lakes and the plains,
Wherever he dream, under mountain or stream,
　　The Spirit he loves remains;
And I all the while bask in heaven's blue smile,
　　Whilst he is dissolving in rains.

The sanguine sunrise, with his meteor eyes,
　　And his burning plumes outspread,
Leaps on the back of my sailing rack
　　When the morning-star shines dead,
As on the jag of a mountain crag,
　　Which an earthquake rocks and swings,
An eagle alit one moment may sit
　　In the light of its golden wings.
And when Sunset may breathe, from the lit sea
　　　beneath
　　Its ardors of rest and of love,
And the crimson pall of eve may fall
　　From the depth of heaven above,
With wings folded I rest, on mine airy nest,
　　As still as a brooding dove.

That orbèd maiden with white fire laden,
　　Whom mortals call the moon,
Glides glimmering o'er my fleece-like floor,
　　By the midnight breezes strewn;
And wherever the beat of her unseen feet,
　　Which only the angels hear,

May have broken the woof of my tent's thin roof,
    The stars peep behind her and peer;
And I laugh to see them whirl and flee,
    Like a swarm of golden bees,
When I widen the rent in my wind-built tent,
    Till the calm rivers, lakes, and seas,
Like strips of the sky fallen through me on high,
    Are each paved with the moon and these.

I bind the sun's throne with the burning zone,
    And the moon's with a girdle of pearl;
The volcanoes are dim, and the stars reel and swim,
    When the whirlwinds my banner unfurl.
From cape to cape, with a bridge-like shape,
    Over a torrent sea,
Sunbeam-proof, I hang like a roof,
    The mountains its columns be.
The triumphal arch through which I march
    With hurricane, fire, and snow,
When the powers of the air are chained to my chair,
    Is the million-colored bow;
The sphere-fire above its soft colors wove,
    While the moist earth was laughing below.

I am the daughter of earth and water,
    And the nursling of the sky:
I pass through the pores of the ocean and shores;
    I change, but I cannot die.
For after the rain when with never a stain,
    The pavilion of heaven is bare,
And the winds and sunbeams with their convex
    gleams,
    Build up the blue dome of air,

I silently laugh at my own cenotaph,
　　And out of the caverns of rain,
Like a child from the womb, like a ghost from the
　　　　tomb,
　　I arise and unbuild it again.

THE RECOLLECTION

By Percy Bysshe Shelley

NOW the last day of many days,
　　All beautiful and bright as
　　　　thou,
　　The loveliest and the last, is
　　　　dead,
　　Rise, Memory, and write its
　　　　praise!
Up, do thy wonted work! come, trace
　　The epitaph of glory fled, —
For now the Earth has changed its face,
　　A frown is on the Heaven's brow.

We wandered to the pine forest
　　That skirts the Ocean's foam;
The lightest wind was in its nest,
　　The tempest in its home.
The whispering waves were half asleep,
　　The clouds were gone to play,
And on the bosom of the deep
　　The smile of Heaven lay;

It seemed as if the hour were one
    Sent from beyond the skies,
Which scattered from above the sun
    A light of Paradise.

We paused amid the pines that stood
    The giants of the waste,
Tortured by storms to shapes as rude
    As serpents interlaced,
And soothed by every azure breath
    That under heaven is blown,
To harmonies and hues beneath,
    As tender as its own;
Now all the tree-tops lay asleep,
    Like green waves on the sea,
As still as in the silent deep
    The ocean woods may be.

How calm it was! — the silence there
    By such a chain was bound,
That even the busy woodpecker
    Made stiller by her sound
The inviolable quietness;
    The breath of peace we drew
With its soft motion made not less
    The calm that round us grew.
There seemed from the remotest seat
    Of the white mountain waste,
To the soft flower beneath our feet,
    A magic circle traced, —

A spirit interfused around,
    A thrilling silent life,

To momentary peace it bound
   Our mortal nature's strife; —
And still I felt the centre of
   The magic circle there
Was one fair Form that filled with love
   The lifeless atmosphere.

We paused beside the pools that lie
   Under the forest bough,
Each seemed as 'twere a little sky
   Gulphed in a world below;
A firmament of purple light
   Which in the dark earth lay,
More boundless than the depth of night,
   And purer than the day —
In which the lovely forests grew
   As in the upper air,
More perfect both in shape and hue
   Than any spreading there.

There lay the glade and neighboring lawn,
   And through the dark green wood
The white sun twinkling like the dawn
   Out of a speckled cloud.
Sweet views which in our world above
   Can never well be seen,
Were imaged by the water's love
   Of that fair forest green.
And all was interfused beneath
   With an elysian glow,
An atmosphere without a breath,
   A softer day below.

Like one beloved the scene had lent
 To the dark water's breast,
Its every leaf and lineament
 With more than truth exprest;
Until an envious wind crept by,
 Like an unwelcome thought,
Which from the mind's too faithful eye
 Blots one dear image out.
Though thou art ever fair and kind,
 The forests ever green,
Less oft is peace in Shelley's mind
 Than calm in waters seen.

THE INVITATION.

By Percy Bysshe Shelley

EST and brightest, come away!
Fairer far than this fair Day,
Which, like thee to those in
 sorrow
Comes to bid a sweet good-mor-
 row
To the rough Year just awake
In its cradle on the brake.
The brightest hour of unborn Spring
Through the winter wandering,
Found, it seems, the halcyon Morn
To hoar February born;
Bending from Heaven, in azure mirth,
It kissed the forehead of the Earth,

And smiled upon the silent sea,
And bade the frozen streams be free,
And waked to music all their fountains,
And breathed upon the frozen mountains,
And like a prophetess of May
Strewed flowers upon the barren way,
Making the wintry world appear
Like one on whom thou smilest, dear.

Away, away, from men and towns,
To the wild wood and the downs —
To the silent wilderness
Where the soul need not repress
Its music lest it should not find
An echo in another's mind,
While the touch of Nature's art
Harmonizes heart to heart.

Radiant Sister of the Day,
Awake! arise! and come away!
To the wild woods and the plains,
And the pools where winter rains
Image all their roof of leaves,
Where the pine its garland weaves
Of sapless green and ivy dun
Round stems that never kiss the sun;
Where the lawns and pastures be,
And the sand-hills of the sea; —
Where the melting hoar-frost wets
The daisy-star that never sets,
And wind-flowers and violets,
Which yet join not scent to hue,
Crown the pale year weak and new;

When the night is left behind
In the deep east, dun and blind,
And the blue noon is over us,
And the multitudinous
Billows murmur at our feet,
Where the earth and ocean meet,
And all things seem only one
In the universal sun.

TO THE RAINBOW.

By Thomas Campbell

TRIUMPHAL arch, that fill'st
the sky
When storms prepare to part,
I ask not proud philosophy
To teach me what thou art.

Still seem as to my childhood's
sight,
A midway station given,
For happy spirits to alight
Betwixt the earth and heaven.

Can all that optics teach unfold
Thy form to please me so,
As when I dreamed of gems and gold
Hid in thy radiant bow?

And yet, fair bow, no fabling dreams,
But words of the Most High,
Have told why first thy robe of beams
Was woven in the sky.

When o'er the green, undeluged earth
   Heaven's covenant thou didst shine,
How came the world's gray fathers forth
   To watch thy sacred sign!

And when its yellow lustre smiled
   O'er mountains yet untrod,
Each mother held aloft her child
   To bless the bow of God.

Methinks, thy jubilee to keep,
   The first-made anthem rang
On earth, delivered from the deep,
   And the first poet sang.

The earth to thee her incense yields,
   The lark thy welcome sings,
When, glittering in the freshened fields,
   The snowy mushroom springs.

How glorious is thy girdle cast
   O'er mountain, tower, and town,
Or mirrored in the ocean vast,
   A thousand fathoms down!

As fresh in yon horizon dark,
   As young thy beauties seem,
As when the eagle from the ark
   First sported in thy beam.

For, faithful to its sacred page,
   Heaven still rebuilds thy span;
Nor lets the type grow pale with age,
   That first spoke peace to man.

THE BEECH TREE'S PETITION

By Thomas Campbell

LEAVE this barren spot to me!
Spare, w o o d m a n, spare the
    beechen tree!
Though bush or floweret never
    grow
My dark unwarming shade be-
    low;
Nor summer bud perfume the dew
Of rosy blush, or yellow hue!
Nor fruits of autumn, blossom-born,
My green and glossy leaves adorn;
Nor murmuring tribes from me derive
Th' ambrosial amber of the hive;
Yet leave this barren spot to me:
Spare, woodman, spare the beechen tree!

Thrice twenty summers I have seen
The sky grow bright, the forest green;
And many a wintry wind have stood
In bloomless, fruitless solitude,
Since childhood in my pleasant bower
First spent its sweet and sportive hour;
Since youthful lovers in my shade
Their vows of truth and rapture made;
And on my trunk's surviving frame
Carv'd many a long-forgotten name.
Oh! by the sighs of gentle sound,
First breathed upon this sacred ground;

By all that Love has whisper'd here,
Or beauty heard with ravish'd ear;
As Love's own altar honour me :
Spare, woodman, spare the beechen tree !

SOLITUDE

By Lord Byron

(From " Childe Harold.")

THERE is a pleasure in the pathless woods,
There is a rapture on the lonely shore,
There is society where none intrudes,
By the deep Sea, and music in its roar:
I love not Man the less, but Nature more,
From these our interviews, in which I steal
From all I may be, or have been before,
To mingle with the Universe, and feel
What I can ne'er express, yet cannot all conceal.

Roll on, thou deep and dark-blue Ocean — roll !
Ten thousand fleets sweep over thee in vain ;
Man marks the earth with ruin — his control
Stops with the shore ; upon the watery plain
The wrecks are all thy deed, nor doth remain
A shadow of man's ravage, save his own,
When, for a moment, like a drop of rain,
He sinks into thy depths with bubbling groan,
Without a grave, unknell'd, uncoffin'd, and unknown.

NIGHT

By Lord Byron

(From " Childe Harold.")

'TIS night, when Meditation bids
    us feel
We once have loved, though
    love is at an end :
The heart, lone mourner of its
    baffled zeal,
Though friendless now, will
    dream it had a friend.
Who with the weight of years would wish to
    bend,
When Youth itself survives young Love and
    Joy ?
Alas ! when mingling souls forget to blend,
Death hath but little left him to destroy !
Ah ! happy years ! once more who would not be
    a boy ?

Thus bending o'er the vessel's laving side,
To gaze on Dian's wave-reflected sphere,
The soul forgets her schemes of hope and pride,
And flies unconscious o'er each backward year.
None are so desolate but something dear,
Dearer than self, possesses or possessed
A thought, and claims the homage of a tear ;
A flashing pang ! of which the weary breast
Would still, albeit in vain, the heavy heart divest.

To sit on rocks, to muse o'er flood and fell,
To slowly trace the forest's shady scene,
Where things that own not man's dominion dwell,
And mortal foot hath ne'er or rarely been ;
To climb the trackless mountain all unseen,
With the wild flock that never needs a fold ;
Alone o'er steeps and foaming falls to lean ;
This is not solitude ; 't is but to hold
Converse with Nature's charms, and view her
           stores unrolled.

But midst the crowd, the hum, the shock of men
To hear, to see, to feel, and to possess,
And roam along, the world's tired denizen,
With none who bless us, none whom we can bless ;
Minions of splendour shrinking from distress !
None that, with kindred consciousness endued,
If we were not, would seem to smile the less
Of all that flatter'd, follow'd, sought, and sued ;
This is to be alone ; this, this is solitude !

SONNET

By *William Shakespeare*

FULL many a glorious morning have I seen
    Flatter the mountain-tops with sovereign eye,
    Kissing with golden face the meadows green,
Gilding pale treams with heavenly alchemy.
Anon permit the basest clouds to ride
With ugly rack on his celestial face,
And from the forlorn world his visage hide,
Stealing unseen to west with this disgrace :

Even so my sun one early morn did shine
With all triumphant splendor on my brow;
But out! alack! he was but one hour mine,
The region cloud hath mask'd him from me now.
Yet him for this my love no whit disdaineth;
Suns of the world may stain, when heaven's sun
        staineth.

MOONLIGHT

By *William Shakespeare*

 OW sweet the moonlight sleeps
    upon this bank!
Here will we sit, and let the
    sounds of music
Creep in your ears: soft still-
    ness, and the night,
Become the touches of sweet
    harmony.

Sit, Jessica: look, how the floor of heaven
Is thick inlaid with patines of bright gold:
There's not the smallest orb which thou behold'st,
But in his motion like an angel sings,
Still quiring to the young-ey'd cherubims.

FLOWERS

By *William Shakespeare*

(From "Winter Night's Tale.")

O Proserpina,
For the flowers now, that frighted, thou let'st fall
From Dis's wagon! daffodils,
That come before the swallow dares, and take
The winds of March with beauty; violets dim,
But sweeter than the lids of Juno's eyes,
Or Cytherea's breath; pale primroses,
That die unmarried, ere they can behold
Bright Phœbus in his strength, a malady
Most incident to maids; bold ox-lips, and
The crown-imperial; lilies of all kinds,
The flower-de-luce being one! O, these I lack,
To make you garlands of; and my sweet friend,
To strew him o'er and o'er!

DOVER CLIFFS

By *William Shakespeare*

(From "King Lear.")

COME on, sir; here's the place:—stand still.
— How fearful
And dizzy 'tis, to cast one's eye so low!
The crows and choughs, that wing the midway air,
Show scarce so gross as beetles: half way down
Hangs one that gathers samphire; dreadful trade!
Methinks he seems no bigger than his head:

The fishermen, that walk upon the beach,
Appear like mice; and yond' tall anchoring bark
Diminish'd to her cock; her cock, a buoy
Almost too small for sight: the murmuring surge,
That on the unnumber'd idle pebbles chafes,
Cannot be heard so high:— I'll look no more;
Lest my brain turn, and the deficient sight
Topple down headlong.

THE STORMY PETREL

By Bryan Waller Procter ("*Barry Cornwall*")

THOUSAND miles from land
are we,
Tossing about on the roaring
sea;
From billow to bounding billow
cast,
Like fleecy snow on the stormy
blast:
The sails are scatter'd abroad, like weeds,
The strong masts shake like quivering reeds,
The mighty cables, and iron chains,
The hull, which all earthly strength disdains,
They strain and they crack, and hearts like stone
Their natural hard, proud strength disown.

Up and down! Up and down!
From the base of the wave to the billow's crown,
And midst the flashing and feathery foam
The Stormy Petrel finds a home,—

A home, if such a place may be,
For her who lives on the wide, wide sea,
On the craggy ice, in the frozen air,
And only seeketh her rocky lair
To warm her young, and to teach them spring
At once o'er the waves on their stormy wing.

O'er the Deep!   O'er the Deep!
Where the whale, and the shark, and the sword-fish
          sleep,
Outflying the blast and the driving rain,
The Petrel telleth her tale — in vain;
For the mariner curseth the warning bird
Who bringeth him news of the storms unheard!
Ah! thus does the prophet, of good or ill,
Meet hate from the creatures he serveth still:
Yet he ne'er falters: — So, Petrel! spring
Once more o'er the waves on thy stormy wing!

THE SEA

By Bryan Waller Procter ("Barry Cornwall")

THE sea! the sea! the open sea!
    The blue, the fresh, the ever free!
    Without a mark, without a bound,
It runneth the earth's wide regions round;
It plays with the clouds; it mocks the skies;
Or like a cradled creature lies.

I'm on the sea!   I'm on the sea!
I am where I would ever be;

With the blue above, and the blue below,
And silence wheresoe'er I go;
If a storm should come and awake the deep,
What matter? *I* shall ride and sleep.

I love, O, how I love to ride
On the fierce, foaming, bursting tide,
When every mad wave drowns the moon
Or whistles aloft his tempest tune,
And tells how goeth the world below,
And why the sou'west blasts do blow.

I never was on the dull, tame shore,
But I lov'd the great sea more and more,
And backwards flew to her billowy breast,
Like a bird that seeketh its mother's nest;
And a mother she was, and is, to me;
For I was born on the open sea!

The waves were white, and red the morn,
In the noisy hour when I was born;
And the whale it whistled, the porpoise roll'd,
And the dolphins bared their backs of gold;
And never was heard such an outcry wild
As welcom'd to life the ocean-child!

I've liv'd since then, in calm and strife,
Full fifty summers, a sailor's life,
With wealth to spend and a power to range,
But never have sought nor sighed for change;
And Death, whenever he comes to me,
Shall come on the wild, unbounded sea!

THE OWL

By Bryan Waller Procter ("Barry Cornwall")

N the hollow tree, in the old
gray tower,
The spectral Owl doth dwell;
Dull, hated, despised in the sun-
shine hour,
But at dusk he's abroad and
well!
Not a bird of the forest e'er mates with him;
All mock him outright, by day;
But at night, when the woods grow still and dim,
The boldest will shrink away!
O, when the night falls, and roosts the fowl,
Then, then, is the reign of the Horned Owl!

And the Owl hath a bride, who is fond and bold,
And loveth the wood's deep gloom;
And, with eyes like the shine of the moonstone cold,
She awaiteth her ghastly groom;
Not a feather she moves, not a carol she sings,
As she waits in her tree so still;
But when her heart heareth his flapping wings,
She hoots out her welcome shrill!
O — when the moon shines, and dogs do howl,
Then, then, is the joy of the Horned Owl!

Mourn not for the Owl, nor his gloomy plight;
The Owl hath his share of good:
If a prisoner he be in the broad daylight,
He is lord in the dark greenwood!

Nor lonely the bird, nor his ghastly mate —
    They are each unto each a pride ;
Thrice fonder, perhaps, since a strange, dark fate
    Hath rent them from all beside !
      So, when the night falls, and dogs do howl,
      Sing, Ho ! for the reign of the Horned Owl !
        We know not alway
        Who are kings by day,
      But the king of the night is the bold brown Owl !

DARWINISM

By Mrs. Darmsteter (A. Mary F. Robinson)

HEN first the unflowering Fern-
    forest,
Shadowed the dim lagoons of old,
A vague unconscious long un-
    rest
Swayed the great fronds of green
    and gold.

Until the flexible stems grew rude,
    The fronds began to branch and bower,
And lo ! upon the unblossoming wood
    There breaks a dawn of apple-flower.

Then on the fruitful Forest-boughs
    For ages long the unquiet ape
Swung happy in his airy house
    And plucked the apple and sucked the grape.

Until in him at length there stirred
 The old, unchanged, remote distress,
That pierced his world of wind and bird
 With some divine unhappiness.

Not Love, nor the wild fruits he sought;
 Nor the fierce battles of his clan
Could still the unborn and aching thought
 Until the brute became the man.

Long since. . . And now the same unrest
 Goads to the same invisible goal,
Till some new gift, undreamed, unguessed,
 End the new travail of the soul.

SCYTHE SONG

By *Andrew Lang*

MOWERS, weary and brown, and
  blithe,
  What is the word methinks ye
  know,
 Endless over-word that the Scythe
  Sings to the blades of the grass
  below ?
Scythes that swing in the grass and clover,
 Something, still, they say as they pass;
What is the word that, over and over,
 Sings the Scythe to the flowers and grass ?

Hush, ah hush, the Scythes are saying,
  Hush, and heed not, and fall asleep;
Hush, they say to the grasses swaying,
  Hush, they sing to the clover deep!
Hush — 'tis the lullaby Time is singing —
  Hush, and heed not, for all things pass,
Hush, ah hush! and the Scythes are swinging
  Over the clover, over the grass!

THE CROCUS

By Harriet Eleanor Hamilton King

UT of the frozen earth below,
  Out of the melting of the
    snow,
    No flower, but a film, I push
      to light;
  No stem, no bud, — yet I have
    burst
The bars of winter, I am the first,
  O Sun, to greet thee out of the night!

Bare are the branches, cold is the air,
Yet it is fire at the heart I bear,
  I come, a flame that is fed by none:
The summer hath blossoms for her delight,
Thick and dewy and waxen-white,
  Thou seest me golden, O golden Sun!

Deep in the warm sleep underground
Life is still, and the peace profound :
   Yet a beam that pierced, and a thrill that smote
Call'd me and drew me from far away ; —
I rose, I came, to the open day
   I have won, unshelter'd, alone, remote.

No bee strays out to greet me at morn,
I shall die ere the butterfly is born,
   I shall hear no note of the nightingale ;
The swallow will come at the break of green,
He will never know that I have been
   Before him here when the world was pale.

They will follow, the rose with the thorny stem,
The hyacinth stalk, — soft airs for them ;
   They shall have strength, I have but love :
They shall not be tender as I, —
Yet I fought here first, to bloom, to die,
   To shine in his face who shines above.

O Glory of heaven, O Ruler of morn,
O Dream that shap'd me, and I was born
   In thy likeness, starry, and flower of flame ;
I lie on the earth, and to thee look up,
Into thy image will grow my cup,
   Till a sunbeam dissolve it into the same.

TO A MOUSE

ON TURNING HER UP IN HER NEST WITH THE
PLOUGH, NOVEMBER, 1785

By *Robert Burns*

WEE, sleekit, cow'rin', tim'rous
    beastie,
O, what a p a n i c ' s in thy
    breastie!
Thou need na start awa sae
    hasty,
      Wi' bickering brattle!
I wad be laith to rin an' chase thee,
      Wi' murd'ring prattle!

I'm truly sorry man's dominion
Has broken Nature's social union,
An' justifies that ill opinion,
      Which makes thee startle
At me, thy poor earth-born companion,
      An' fellow-mortal!

I doubt na, whiles, but thou may thieve;
What then? poor beastie, thou maun live!
A daimen-icker in a thrave
      'S a sma' request;
I'll get a blessin' wi' the lave,
      And never miss't!

Thy wee bit housie, too, in ruin!
Its silly wa's the win's are strewin!

An' naething, now, to big a new ane,
      O' foggage green!
An' bleak December's winds ensuin',
      Baith snell an' keen!

Thou saw the fields laid bare and waste,
An' weary winter comin' fast,
An' cozie here, beneath the blast,
      Thou thought to dwell,
Till crash! the cruel coulter past,
      Out through thy cell.

That wee bit heap o' leaves an' stibble
Has cost thee mony a weary nibble!
Now thou's turn'd out, for a' thy trouble,
      But house or hald,
To thole the winter's sleety dribble,
      An' cranreuch cauld!

But, Mousie, thou art no thy lane,
In proving foresight may be vain:
The best laid schemes o' mice an' men
      Gang aft a-gley,
An' lea'e us nought but grief an' pain,
      For promis'd joy.

Still thou art blest, compar'd wi' me!
The present only toucheth thee:
But, Och! I backward cast my e'e
      On prospects drear!
An' forward, tho' I canna see,
      I guess an' fear!

AFTON WATER

By *Robert Burns*

FLOW gently, sweet Afton,
    among thy green braes,
Flow gently, I'll sing thee a song
    in thy praise;
My Mary's asleep by thy mur-
    muring stream,
Flow gently, sweet Afton, dis-
    turb not her dream.

Thou stock-dove whose echo resounds thro' the
        glen,
Ye wild whistling blackbirds in yon thorny den,
Thou green-crested lapwing, thy screaming forbear,
I charge you disturb not my slumbering fair.

How lofty, sweet Afton, thy neighboring hills,
Far mark'd with the courses of clear winding rills;
There daily I wander as noon rises high,
My flocks and my Mary's sweet cot in my eye.

How pleasant thy banks and green valleys below,
Where wild in the woodlands the primroses blow!
There oft as mild ev'ning weeps over the lea,
The sweet-scented birk shades my Mary and me.

Thy crystal stream, Afton, how lovely it glides,
And winds by the cot where my Mary resides;
How wanton thy waters her snowy feet lave,
As gathering sweet flow'rets she stems thy clear
        wave!

Flow gently, sweet Afton, among thy green braes;
Flow gently, sweet river, the theme of my lays;
My Mary's asleep by thy murmuring stream,
Flow gently, sweet Afton, disturb not her dream.

ON SEEING A WOUNDED HARE LIMP BY ME

WHICH A FELLOW HAD JUST SHOT AT

By Robert Burns

I

INHUMAN man! curse on thy
   barb'rous art,
   And blasted be thy murder-
      aiming eye;
   May never pity soothe thee
      with a sigh,
Nor ever pleasure glad thy cruel
   heart!

II

Go live, poor wanderer of the wood and field,
   The bitter little that of life remains;
   No more the thickening brakes and verdant
      plains
To thee shall home, or food, or pastime yield.

III

Seek, mangled wretch, some place of wonted rest,
   No more of rest, but now thy dying bed!
   The sheltering rushes whistling o'er thy head,
The cold earth with thy bloody bosom prest.

IV

Oft as by winding Nith, I, musing, wait
　　The sober eve, or hail the cheerful dawn,
　　I'll miss thee sporting o'er the dewy lawn,
And curse the ruffian's aim, and mourn thy hapless
　　　　fate.

"AGAIN REJOICING NATURE SEES"

By Robert Burns

AGAIN rejoicing Nature sees
　　Her robe assume its vernal
　　　hues,
Her leafy locks wave in the
　　breeze,
　　All freshly steep'd in morning
　　dews.

CHORUS

And maun I still on Menie doat,
　　And bear the scorn that's in her e'e?
For it's jet, jet black, an' it's like a hawk,
　　An' it winna let a body be!

In vain to me the cowslips blaw,
　　In vain to me the vi'lets spring;
In vain to me in glen or shaw,
　　The mavis and the lintwhite sing.
　　　　And maun I still, etc.

The merry ploughboy cheers his team,
 Wi' joy the tentie seedsman stalks,
But life to me's a weary dream,
 A dream of ane that never wauks.

  And maun I still, etc.

The wanton coot the water skims,
 Amang the reeds the ducklings cry,
The stately swan majestic swims,
 And everything is blest but I.

  And maun I still, etc.

The sheep-herd steeks his faulding slap,
 And owre the moorlands whistles shill,
Wi' wild, unequal, wand'ring step
 I meet him on the dewy hill.

  And maun I still, etc.

And when the lark, 'tween light and dark,
 Blythe waukens by the daisy's side,
And mounts and sings on flittering wings,
 A woe-worn ghaist I hameward glide.

  And maun I still, etc.

Come Winter, with thine angry howl,
 And raging bend the naked tree;
Thy gloom will soothe my cheerless soul,
 When Nature all is sad like me!
And maun I still on Menie doat,
 And bear the scorn that's in her e'e?
For it's jet, jet black, an' it's like a hawk,
 An' it winna let a body be!

TO A MOUNTAIN DAISY

ON TURNING ONE DOWN WITH THE PLOUGH, IN
APRIL, 1786

By Robert Burns

WEE, modest, crimson-tippèd
  flow'r,
Thou's met me in an evil
  hour;
For I maun crush amang the
  stoure
      Thy slender stem.
To spare thee now is past my pow'r,
      Thou bonie gem.

Alas! it's no thy neeber sweet,
The bonie lark, companion meet,
Bending thee 'mang the dewy weet!
      Wi' spreckl'd breast!
When upward-springing, blythe, to greet,
      The purpling east.

Cauld blew the bitter-biting north
Upon thy early, humble birth;
Yet cheerfully thou glinted forth
      Amid the storm,
Scarce rear'd above the parent-earth
      Thy tender form.

The flaunting flow'rs our gardens yield,
High shelt'ring woods and wa's maun shield;

But thou, beneath the random bield
           O' clod or stane,
Adorns the histie stibble-field,
           Unseen, alane.

There, in thy scanty mantle clad,
Thy snawie bosom sun-ward spread,
Thou lifts thy unassuming head
           In humble guise ;
But now the share uptears thy bed,
           And low thou lies !

Such is the fate of artless Maid,
Sweet flow'ret of the rural shade !
By love's simplicity betray'd,
           And guileless trust,
Till she, like thee, all soil'd, is laid
           Low i' the dust.

Such is the fate of simple Bard,
On Life's rough ocean luckless starr'd !
Unskilful he to note the card
           Of prudent lore,
Till billows rage, and gales blow hard,
           And whelm him o'er !

Such fate to suffering worth is giv'n,
Who long with wants and woes has striv'n,
By human pride or cunning driv'n
           To mis'ry's brink,
Till, wrench'd of ev'ry stay but Heav'n,
           He, ruin'd, sink !

Ev'n thou who mourn'st the Daisy's fate,
That fate is thine — no distant date;
Stern Ruin's ploughshare drives elate,
      Full on thy bloom,
Till crush'd beneath the furrow's weight,
      Shall be thy doom!

BONNIE DOON

By Robert Burns

YE banks and braes o' bonnie Doon
    How can ye bloom sae fresh
      and fair?
How can ye chaunt, ye little
    birds,
    And I sae weary, fu' of care?
Thou'lt break my heart, thou
    warbling bird,
That wantons through the flow'ry thorn,
Thou mindst me o' departed joys,
    Departed never to return.

Oft hae I rov'd by bonnie Doon,
    To see the rose and woodbine twine;
When ilka bird sang o' its love,
    And fondly sae did I o' mine.
Wi' lightsome heart I pu'd a rose,
    Fu' sweet upon its thorny tree;
But my fause lover stole my rose,
    And, ah! he left the thorn wi' me.

SPRING SONG IN THE CITY

By Robert Buchanan

HO remains in London,
  In the streets with me,
Now that Spring is blowing
  Warm winds from the sea;
Now that trees grow green and
    tall,
  Now the sun shines mellow,
And with moist primroses all
  English lanes are yellow?

Little barefoot maiden,
  Selling violets blue,
Hast thou ever pictur'd
  Where the sweetlings grew?
Oh, the warm wild woodland ways,
  Deep in dewy grasses,
Where the wind-blown shadow strays,
  Scented as it passes!

Pedlar breathing deeply,
  Toiling into town,
With the dusty highway
  You are dusky brown;
Hast thou seen by daisied leas,
  And by rivers flowing,
Lilac-ringlets which the breeze
  Loosens lightly blowing?

Out of yonder wagon
  Pleasant hay-scents float,

He who drives it carries
    A daisy in his coat:
Oh, the English meadows, fair
    Far beyond all praises!
Freckled orchids everywhere
    'Mid the snow of daisies!

Now in busy silence
    Broods the nightingale,
Choosing his love's dwelling
    In a dimpled dale;
Round the leafy bower they raise
    Rose-trees wild are springing;
Underneath, thro' the green haze,
    Bounds the brooklet singing.

And his love is silent
    As a bird can be,
For the red buds only
    Fill the red rose-tree;
Just as buds and blossoms blow
    He'll begin his tune,
When all is green and roses glow
    Underneath the moon.

Nowhere in the valleys
    Will the wind be still,
Everything is waving,
    Wagging at his will:
Blows the milkmaid's kirtle clean,
    With her hand press'd on it;
Lightly o'er the hedge so green
    Blows the ploughboy's bonnet.

Oh, to be a-roaming
    In an English dell!
Every nook is wealthy,
    All the world looks well,
Tinted soft the Heavens glow,
    Over Earth and Ocean,
Waters flow, breezes blow,
    All is light and motion!

TO A HUMMING BIRD IN A GARDEN

By George Murray

LITHE playmate of the Summer
        time,
    Admiringly I greet thee;
Born in old England's misty
        clime,
    I scarcely hoped to meet
        thee.

Com'st thou from forests of Peru,
    Or from Brazil's savannahs,
Where flowers of every dazzling hue
    Flaunt, gorgeous as Sultanas?

Thou scannest me with doubtful gaze,
    Suspicious little stranger!
Fear not, thy burnished wings may blaze
    Secure from harm or danger.

Now here, now there, thy flash is seen,
  Like some stray sunbeam darting,
With scarce a second's space between
  Its coming and departing.

Mate of the bird that lives sublime
  In Pat's immortal blunder,
Spied in two places at a time,
  Thou challengest our wonder.

Suspended by thy slender bill,
  Sweet blooms thou lov'st to rifle;
The subtle perfumes they distil
  Might well thy being stifle.

Surely the honey-dew of flowers
  Is slightly alcoholic,
Or why, through burning August hours,
  Dost thou pursue thy frolic?

What though thy throatlet never rings
  With music, soft or stirring;
Still, like a spinning-wheel, thy wings
  Incessantly are whirring.

How dearly I would love to see
  Thy tiny *cara sposa*,
As full of sensibility
  As any coy mimosa!

They say, when hunters track her nest
  Where two warm pearls are lying,
She boldly fights, though sore distrest,
  And sends the brigands flying.

What dainty epithets thy tribes
  Have won from men of science!
Pedantic and poetic scribes
  For once are in alliance.

Crested Coquette, and Azure Crown,
  Sun Jewel, Ruby-Throated,
With Flaming Topaz, Crimson Down,
  Are names that may be quoted.

Such titles aim to paint the hues
  That on the darlings glitter,
And were we for a week to muse,
  We scarce could light on fitter.

Farewell, bright bird! I envy thee,
  Gay rainbow-tinted rover;
Would that my life, like thine, were free
  From care till all is over!

THE SKYLARK

By Frederick Tennyson

HOW the blithe Lark runs up the golden stair
    That leans thro' cloudy gates from Heaven
      to Earth,
And all alone in the empyreal air
  Fills it with jubilant sweet songs of mirth;
    How far he seems, how far
      With the light upon his wings,
    Is it a bird, or star
      That shines, and sings?

What matter if the days be dark and frore,
    That sunbeam tells of other days to be,
And singing in the light that floods him o'er
        In joy he overtakes Futurity;
            Under cloud-arches vast
                He peeps, and sees behind
            Great Summer coming fast
                Adown the wind!

And now he dives into a rainbow's rivers,
    In streams of gold and purple he is drown'd,
Shrilly the arrows of his song he shivers,
        As tho' the stormy drops were turn'd to sound;
            And now he issues thro',
                He scales a cloudy tower,
            Faintly, like falling dew,
                His fast notes shower.

Let every wind be hush'd, that I may hear
    The wondrous things he tells the World below,
Things that we dream of he is watching near,
        Hopes that we never dream'd he would bestow;
            Alas! the storm hath roll'd
                Back the gold gates again,
            Or surely he had told
                All Heaven to men!

So the victorious Poet sings alone,
    And fills with light his solitary home,
And thro' that glory sees new worlds foreshown,
    And hears high songs, and triumphs yet to
        come;

He waves the air of Time
  With thrills of golden chords,
And makes the world to climb
  On linkèd words.

What if his hair be gray, his eyes be dim,
  If wealth forsake him, and if friends be cold,
Wonder unbars her thousand gates to him,
  Truth never fails, nor Beauty waxes old;
    More than he tells his eyes
      Behold, his spirit hears,
    Of grief, and joy, and sighs
      'Twixt joy and tears.

Blest is the man who with the sound of song
  Can charm away the heartache, and forget
The frost of Penury, and the stings of Wrong,
  And drown the fatal whisper of Regret!
    Darker are the abodes
      Of Kings, tho' his be poor,
    While Fancies, like the Gods,
      Pass thro' his door.

Singing thou scalest Heaven upon thy wings,
  Thou liftest a glad heart into the skies;
He maketh his own sunrise, while he sings,
  And turns the dusty Earth to Paradise;
    I see thee sail along
      Far up the sunny streams,
    Unseen, I hear his song,
      I see his dreams.

A GLEE FOR WINTER

By Alfred Domett

ENCE, rude Winter! crabbed old fellow,
Never merry, never mellow!
Well-a day! in rain and snow
What will keep one's heart aglow?
Groups of kinsmen, old and young,
Oldest they old friends among;
Groups of friends, so old and true
That they seem our kinsmen too;
These all merry all together
Charm away chill Winter weather.

What will kill this dull old fellow?
Ale that's bright, and wine that's mellow!
Dear old songs for ever new;
Some true love, and laughter too;
Pleasant wit, and harmless fun,
And a dance when day is done.
Music, friends so true and tried,
Whisper'd love by warm fireside,
Mirth at all times all together,
Makes sweet May of Winter weather.

HOME-THOUGHTS FROM ABROAD

By Robert Browning

I

H, to be in England now that
  April's there,
And whoever wakes in England
  sees, some morning, unaware,
That the lowest boughs and the
  brush-wood sheaf
Round the elm-tree bole are in
  tiny leaf,
While the chaffinch sings on the orchard bough
In England — now!

II

And after April, when May follows,
And the white-throat builds, and all the swallows!
Hark, where my blossomed pear-tree in the hedge
Leans to the field and scatters on the clover
Blossoms and dewdrops — at the bent spray's
    edge —
That's the wise thrush; he sings each song twice
    over
Lest you should think he never could recapture
The first fine careless rapture!
And though the fields look rough with hoary **dew,**
All will be gay when noontide wakes anew
The buttercups, the little children's dower,
Far brighter than this gaudy melon-flower!

BY THE FIRESIDE

By Robert Browning

A TURN, and we stand in the
    heart of things;
    The woods are round us
      heaped and dim;
From slab to slab how it slips
    and springs,
    The thread of water single
      and slim
Through the ravage some torrent brings!

Does it feed the little lake below?
    That speck of white just on its marge
Is Pella; see in the evening glow,
    How sharp the silver spear-heads charge
When Alp meets heaven in snow!

On our other side is the straight-up rock;
    And a path is kept 'twixt the gorge and it
By boulder-stones where lichens mock
    The marks on a moth, and small ferns fit
Their teeth to the polished block.

Oh the sense of the yellow mountain-flowers
    And thorny balls, each three in one,
The chestnuts throw on our path in showers!
    For the drop of the woodland fruit 's begun,
These early November hours,

That crimson the creeper's leaf across
　　Like a splash of blood, intense, abrupt,
O'er a shield else gold from rim to boss,
　　And lay it for show on the fairy-cupped
Elf-needled mat of moss,

By the rose-flesh mushrooms, undivulged
　　Last evening — nay, in to-day's first dew
Yon sudden coral nipple bulged,
　　Where a freaked fawn-colored flaky crew
Of toad-stools peep indulged.

.　　.　　.　　.　　.　　.　　.

And all day long a bird sings there,
　　And a stray sheep drinks at the pond at times;
The place is silent and aware;
　　It has had its scenes, its joys and crimes,
But that is its own affair.

PIPPA PASSES

(From " Pippa Passes ")

By Robert Browning

DAY!
　　Faster and more fast,
　　　　O'er night's brim, day boils at last;
Boils, pure gold, o'er the cloud-cup's brim
Where spurting and suppressed it lay,
For not a froth-flake touched the rim
Of yonder gap in the solid gray
Of the eastern cloud, an hour away;

But forth one wavelet, then another, curled,
Till the whole sunrise, not to be suppressed,
Rose, reddened, and its seething breast
Flickered in bounds, grew gold, then overflowed
    the world.

THE IRISH WOLF-HOUND

(From "The Foray of Con O'Donnell")

By Denis Florence MacCarthy

S fly the shadows o'er the grass,
    He flies with step as light and
        sure,
    He hunts the wolf through Tos-
        tan pass,
    And starts the deer by Lisa-
        noure.
The music of the Sabbath bells,
    O Con! has not a sweeter sound
Than when along the valley swells
    The cry of John Mac Donnell's hound.

His stature tall, his body long,
    His back like night, his breast like snow,
His fore-leg pillar-like and strong,
    His hind-leg like a bended bow;
Rough curling hair, head long and thin,
    His ear a leaf so small and round;
Not Bran, the favorite dog of Fin,
    Could rival John Mac Donnell's hound.

THE FROSTED PANE

By Charles G. D. Roberts

ONE night came Winter noise-
    lessly and leaned
    Against my window-pane.
In the deep stillness of his heart
    convened
    The ghosts of all his slain.

Leaves, and ephemera, and stars of earth,
    And fugitives of grass, —
White spirits loosed from bonds of mortal birth,
    He drew them on the glass.

AUTOCHTHON

By Charles G. D. Roberts

I AM the spirit astir
    To swell the grain,
    When fruitful sons confer
With laboring rain;
I am the life that thrills
    In branch and bloom;
I am the patience of abiding hills,
    The promise masked in doom.

When the sombre lands are wrung,
    And storms are out,
And giant woods give tongue,
    I am the shout;

And when the earth would sleep,
   Wrapped in her snows,
I am the infinite gleam of eyes that keep
   The post of her repose.

I am the hush of calm,
   I am the speed,
The flood-tide's triumphing psalm,
   The marsh-pool's heed;
I work in the rocking roar
   Where cataracts fall;
I flash in the prismy fire that dances o'er
   The dew's ephemeral ball.

I am the voice of wind
   And wave and tree,
Of stern desires and blind,
   Of strength to be;
I am the cry by night
   At point of dawn,
The summoning bugle from the unseen height,
   In cloud and doubt withdrawn.

I am the strife that shapes
   The stature of man,
The pang no hero escapes,
   The blessing, the ban;
I am the hammer that moulds
   The iron of our race,
The omen of God in our blood that a people be-
    holds,
   The foreknowledge veiled in our face.

THE HAWKBIT

By Charles G. D. Roberts

HOW sweetly on the autumn scene,
When haws are red amid the green,
The hawkbit shines with face of cheer,
The favorite of the faltering year!

When days grow short and nights grow cold,
How fairly gleams its eye of gold
On pastured field and grassy hill,
Along the roadside and the rill!

It seems the spirit of a flower,
This offspring of the autumn hour,
Wandering back to earth to bring
Some kindly afterthought of spring.

A dandelion's ghost might so
Amid Elysian meadows blow,
Become more fragile and more fine
Breathing the atmosphere divine.

THE FLIGHT OF THE GEESE

By Charles G. D. Roberts

HEAR the low wind wash the softening snow,
The low tide loiter down the shore. The night,
Full filled with April forecast, hath no light.
The salt wave on the sedge-flat pulses slow.
Through the hid furrows lisp in murmurous flow
The thaw's shy ministers; and hark! The height
Of heaven grows weird and loud with unseen flight
Of strong hosts prophesying as they go!
High through the drenched and hollow night their
    wings
Beat northward hard on winter's trail. The sound
Of their confused and solemn voices, borne
Athwart the dark to their long arctic morn,
Comes with a sanction and an awe profound,
A boding of unknown, foreshadowed things.

WALDEINSAMKEIT

By Ralph Waldo Emerson

I DO not count the hours I spend
In wandering by the sea;
The forest is my loyal friend,
Like God it useth me.

In plains that room for shadows make
    Of skirting hills to lie,
Bound in by streams which give and take
    Their colors from the sky;

Or on the mountain-crest sublime,
    Or down the oaken glade,
O what have I to do with time?
    For this the day was made.

Cities of mortals woe-begone
    Fantastic care derides,
But in the serious landscape lone
    Stern benefit abides.

Sheen will tarnish, honey cloy,
    And merry is only a mask of sad,
But, sober on a fund of joy,
    The woods at heart are glad.

There the great Planter plants
    Of fruitful worlds the grain,
And with a million spells enchants
    The souls that walk in pain.

Still on the seeds of all he made
    The rose of beauty burns;
Through times that wear and forms that fade,
    Immortal youth returns.

The black ducks mounting from the lake,
    The pigeon in the pines,
The bittern's boom, a desert make
    Which no false art refines.

Down in yon watery nook,
  Where bearded mists divide,
The gray old gods whom Chaos knew,
  The sires of Nature, hide.

Aloft, in secret veins of air,
  Blows the sweet breath of song,
O, few to scale those uplands dare,
  Though they to all belong!

See thou bring not to field or stone
  The fancies found in books;
Leave author's eyes, and fetch your own,
  To brave the landscape's looks.

Oblivion here thy wisdom is,
  Thy thrift, the sleep of cares;
For a proud idleness like this
  Crowns all thy mean affairs.

THE HUMBLE-BEE

By Ralph Waldo Emerson

BURLY, dozing humble-bee,
  Where thou art is clime for me.
  Let them sail for Porto Rique,
Far-off heats through seas to seek;
I will follow thee alone,
Thou animated torrid-zone!
Zigzag steerer, desert cheerer,
Let me chase thy waving lines;
Keep me nearer, me thy hearer,
Singing over shrubs and vines.

Insect lover of the sun,
Joy of thy dominion!
Sailor of the atmosphere;
Swimmer through the waves of air;
Voyager of light and noon;
Epicurean of June;
Wait, I prithee, till I come
Within earshot of thy hum, —
All without is martyrdom.

When the south wind, in May days,
With a net of shining haze
Silvers the horizon wall,
And with softness touching all,
Tints the human countenance
With a color of romance,
And infusing subtle heats,
Turns the sod to violets,
Thou, in sunny solitudes,
Rover of the underwoods,
The green silence dost displace
With thy mellow, breezy bass.

Hot midsummer's petted crone,
Sweet to me thy drowsy tone
Tells of countless sunny hours,
Long days, and solid banks of flowers;
Of gulfs of sweetness without bound
In Indian wildernesses found;
Of Syrian peace, immortal leisure,
Firmest cheer, and bird-like pleasure.

Aught unsavory or unclean
Hath my insect never seen;

But violets and bilberry bells,
Maple-sap and daffodels,
Grass with green flag half-mast high,
Succory to match the sky,
Columbine with horn of honey,
Scented fern, and agrimony,
Clover, catchfly, adder's-tongue
And brier-roses, dwelt among;
All beside was unknown waste,
All was picture as he passed.

Wiser far than human seer,
Yellow-breeched philosopher!
Seeing only what is fair,
Sipping only what is sweet,
Thou dost mock at fate and care,
Leave the chaff, and take the wheat.
When the fierce northwestern blast
Cools sea and land so far and fast,
Thou already slumberest deep;
Woe and want thou canst outsleep;
Want and woe, which torture us,
Thy sleep makes ridiculous.

SONG OF NATURE

By Ralph Waldo Emerson

MINE are the night and morning,
The pits of air, the gulf of space,
The sportive sun, the gibbous moon,
The innumerable days.

I hide in the solar glory,
I am dumb in the pealing song,
I rest on the pitch of the torrent,
In slumber I am strong.

No numbers have counted my tallies,
No tribes my house can fill,
I sit by the shining Fount of Life
And pour the deluge still;

And ever by delicate powers
Gathering along the centuries
From race on race the rarest flowers,
My wreath shall nothing miss.

And many a thousand summers
My gardens ripened well,
And light from meliorating stars
With firmer glory fell.

I wrote the past in characters
Of rock and fire the scroll,
The building in the coral sea,
The planting of the coal.

And thefts from satellites and rings
And broken stars I drew,
And out of spent and aged things
I formed the world anew;

What time the gods kept carnival,
Tricked out in star and flower,
And in cramp elf and saurian forms
They swathed their too much power.

Time and Thought were my surveyors,
They laid their courses well,
They boiled the sea, and piled the layers
Of granite, marl and shell.

But he, the man-child glorious, —
Where tarries he the while?
The rainbow shines his harbinger,
The sunset gleams his smile.

My boreal lights leap upward,
Forthright my planets roll,
And still the man-child is not born,
The summit of the whole.

Must time and tide forever run?
Will never my winds go sleep in the west?
Will never my wheels which whirl the sun
And satellites have rest?

Too much of donning and doffing,
Too slow the rainbow fades,
I weary of my robe of snow,
My leaves and my cascades;

I tire of globes and races,
Too long the game is played;
What without him is summer's pomp,
Or winter's frozen shade?

I travail in pain for him,
My creatures travail and wait;
His couriers come by squadrons,
He comes not to the gate.

Twice I have moulded an image,
And thrice outstretched my hand,
Made one of day and one of night
And one of the salt sea-sand.

One in a Judæan manger,
And one by Avon stream,
One over against the mouths of Nile,
And one in the Academe.

I moulded kings and saviors,
And bards o'er kings to rule; —
But fell the starry influence short,
The cup was never full.

Yet whirl the glowing wheels once more,
And mix the bowl again;
Seethe, Fate! the ancient elements,
Heat, cold, wet, dry, and peace, and pain.

Let war and trade and creeds and song
Blend, ripen race on race,
The sunburnt world a man shall breed
Of all the zones and countless days.

No ray is dimmed, no atom worn,
My oldest force is good as new,
And the fresh rose on yonder thorn
Gives back the bending heavens in dew.

THE JOYS OF THE ROAD

By Bliss Carman

OW the joys of the road are chiefly these:
A crimson touch on the hardwood trees;

A vagrant's morning wide and blue,
In early fall, when the wind walks, too;

A shadowy highway cool and brown,
Alluring up and enticing down

From rippled water to dappled swamp,
From purple glory to scarlet pomp;

The outward eye, the quiet will,
And the striding heart from hill to hill;

The tempter apple over the fence;
The cobweb bloom on the yellow quince;

The palish asters along the wood, —
A lyric touch of the solitude;

An open hand, an easy shoe,
And a hope to make the day go through, —

Another to sleep with, and a third,
To wake me up at the voice of a bird;

The resonant far-listening morn,
And the hoarse-whisper of the corn;

The crickets mourning their comrades lost,
In the night's retreat from the gathering frost;

(Or is it their slogan, plaintive and shrill,
As they beat on their corselets, valiant still?)

A hunger fit for the kings of the sea,
And a loaf of bread for Dickon and me;

A thirst like that of the Thirsty Sword,
And a jug of cider on the board;

An idle noon, a bubbling spring,
The sea in the pine-tops murmuring;

A scrap of gossip at the ferry;
A comrade neither glum nor merry,

Asking nothing, revealing naught,
But minting his words from a fund of thought,

A keeper of silence eloquent,
Needy, yet royally well content,

Of the mettled breed, yet abhorring strife,
And full of the mellow juice of life,

A taster of wine, with an eye for a maid,
Never too bold, and never afraid,

Never heart-whole, never heart-sick,
(These are the things I worship in Dick)

No fidget and no reformer, just
A calm observer of ought and must,

A lover of books, but a reader of man,
No cynic and no charlatan,

Who never defers and never demands,
But, smiling, takes the world in his hands, —

Seeing it good as when God first saw
And gave it the weight of his will for law.

And O the joy that is never won,
But follows and follows the journeying sun,

By marsh and tide, by meadow and stream,
A will-o'-the-wind, a light-o'-dream,

Delusion afar, delight anear,
From morrow to morrow, from year to year,

A jack-o'-lantern, a fairy fire,
A dare, a bliss, and a desire!

The racy smell of the forest loam,
When the stealthy, sad-heart leaves go home;

(O leaves, O leaves, I am one with you,
Of the mould and the sun and the wind and the dew!)

The broad gold wake of the afternoon;
The silent fleck of the cold new moon;

The sound of the hollow sea's release
From stormy tumult to starry peace;

With only another league to wend;
And two brown arms at the journey's end!

These are the joys of the open road —
For him who travels without a load.

A MORE ANCIENT MARINER

By Bliss Carman

THE swarthy bee is a buccaneer,
    A burly velveted rover,
    Who loves the booming wind
        in his ear
    As he sails the seas of clover.

A waif of the goblin pirate crew,
    With not a soul to deplore him,
He steers for the open verge of blue
    With the filmy world before him.

His flimsy sails abroad on the wind
    Are shivered with fairy thunder;
On a line that sings to the light of his wings
    He makes for the lands of wonder.

He harries the ports of the Hollyhocks,
    And levies on poor Sweetbrier;
He drinks the whitest wine of Phlox,
    And the Rose is his desire.

He hangs in the Willows a night and a day;
    He rifles the Buckwheat patches;
Then battens his store of pelf galore
    Under the tautest hatches.

He woos the Poppy and weds the Peach,
    Inveigles Daffodilly,
And then like a tramp abandons each
    For the gorgeous Canada Lily.

There's not a soul in the garden world
  But wishes the day were shorter,
When Mariner B. puts out to sea
  With the wind in the proper quarter.

Or, so they say! But I have my doubts;
  For the flowers are only human,
And the valor and gold of a vagrant bold
  Were always dear to woman.

He dares to boast, along the coast,
  The beauty of Highland Heather, —
How he and she, with night on the sea,
  Lay out on the hills together.

He pilfers from every port of the wind,
  From April to golden autumn;
But the thieving ways of his mortal days
  Are those his mother taught him.

His morals are mixed, but his will is fixed;
  He prospers after his kind,
And follows an instinct, compass-sure,
  The philosophers call blind.

And that is why, when he comes to die,
  He'll have an easier sentence
Than some one I know who thinks just so,
  And then leaves room for repentance.

He never could box the compass round;
  He doesn't know port from starboard;
But he knows the gates of the Sundown Straits,
  Where the choicest goods are harbored.

He never could see the Rule of Three,
　　But he knows the rule of thumb
Better than Euclid's, better than yours,
　　Or the teachers' yet to come.

He knows the smell of the hydromel
　　As if two and two were five;
And hides it away for a year and a day
　　In his own hexagonal hive.

Out in the day, hap-hazard, alone,
　　Booms the old vagrant hummer,
With only his whim to pilot him
　　Through the splendid vast of summer.

He steers and steers on the slant of the gale,
　　Like the fiend or Vanderdecken;
And there's never an unknown course to sail
　　But his crazy log can reckon.

He drones along with his rough sea-song
　　And the throat of a salty tar,
This devil-may-care, till he makes his lair
　　By the light of a yellow star.

He looks like a gentleman, lives like a lord,
　　And works like a Trojan hero;
Then loafs all winter upon his hoard,
　　With the mercury at zero.

THE SONG THE ORIOLE SINGS

By *William Dean Howells*

THERE is a bird that comes and
    sings
    In a professor's garden-trees ;
Upon the English oak he swings,
    And tilts and tosses in the
    breeze.

I know his name, I know his note,
    That so with rapture takes my soul ;
Like flame the gold beneath his throat,
    His glossy cope is black as coal.

O oriole, it is the song
    You sang me from the cottonwood,
Too young to feel that I was young,
    Too glad to guess if life were good.

And while I hark, before my door,
    Adown the dusty Concord Road,
The blue Miami flows once more
    As by the cottonwood it flowed.

And on the bank that rises steep,
    And pours a thousand tiny rills,
From death and absence laugh and leap
    My school-mates to their flutter-mills.

The blackbirds jangle in the tops
  Of hoary-antlered sycamores ;
The timorous killdee starts and stops
  Among the drift-wood on the shores.

Below, the bridge — a noonday fear
  Of dust and shadow shot with sun —
Stretches its gloom from pier to pier,
  Far unto alien coasts unknown.

And on these alien coasts, above,
  Where silver ripples break the stream's
Long blue, from some roof-sheltering grove
  A hidden parrot scolds and screams.

Ah, nothing, nothing ! Commonest things :
  A touch, a glimpse, a sound, a breath —
It is a song the oriole sings —
  And all the rest belongs to death.

But oriole, my oriole,
  Were some bright seraph sent from bliss
With songs of heaven to win my soul
  From simple memories such as this,

What could he tell to tempt my ear
  From you ?   What high thing could there be,
So tenderly and sweetly dear
  As my lost boyhood is to me ?

APRIL

By Lloyd Mifflin

(From "The Fields of Dawn.")

AMONG the maple-buds we hear
the tones
  Of April's earliest bees, al-
    though the days
Seemed ruled by Mars. The
  veil of gathering haze
Spread round the silent hills
  in bluest zones.

Deep in the pines the breezes stirred the cones,
  As on we strolled within the wooded ways,
  There where the brook, transilient, softly plays
With muffled plectrum on her harp of stones ;
Onward we pushed amid the yielding green
  And light rebounding of the cedar boughs,
  Until we heard — the forest lanes along,
Above the lingering drift of latest snows —
  The Thrush outpour, from coverts still unseen,
  His rare ebulliency of liquid song !

SUMMER

By Lloyd Mifflin

(From " The Fields of Dawn ")

 OW well we loved, in Summer
  solitude
  To stroll on lonely ridges far
   away,
  Where beeches, with their
   boles of Quaker gray,
  Murmured at times a sylvan
   interlude !
We heard each songster warble near her brood,
 And from the lowland where the mowers lay
 Came now and then faint fragrance from the hay,
 That touched the heart to reminiscent mood.
We peered down wooded steeps, and saw the sun
 Shining in front, tip all the grape-vines wild,
 And edge with light the bowlders' lichened
  groups ;
While, deep within the gorge, the tinkling run
 Coiled through the hollows with its silvered
  loops
 Down to the waiting River, thousand-isled.

AUTUMN

By Lloyd Mifflin

(From " The Fields of Dawn")

THE nearest woodlands wore a
 misty veil ;
From phantom trees we saw
 the last leaf float ;
The hills though near us
 seemed to lie remote,
Wrapped in a balmy vapor,
 golden — pale.
From somewhere hidden in the dreamy dale —
 Latona's sorrow yet within her note —
 Reft of her comrades, o'er the stubbled oat
We heard the calling of the lonely quail.
In the bare corn-field stalked the silent crow ;
 Too faint the breeze to make the grasses sigh,
 And not one carol came from out the sky ;
But o'er the golden gravelly levels low,
 The brook, loquacious, still went lilting by
 As liquidly as Lara, long ago.

GOLDEN CROWN SPARROW OF ALASKA

By John Burroughs

H, minstrel of these borean hills,
    Where twilight hours are long,
I would my boyhood's fragrant days
    Had known thy plaintive song;

Had known thy vest of ashen gray,
  Thy coat of drab and brown,
The bands of jet upon thy head
  That clasp thy golden crown.

We heard thee in the cold White Pass,
  Where cloud and mountain meet,
Again where Muir's glacier shone
  Far spread beneath our feet.

I bask me now on emerald heights
  To catch thy faintest strain,
But cannot tell if in thy lay
  Be more of joy or pain.

Far off behold the snow-white peaks
  Athwart the sea's blue-shade;
Anear there rise green Kadiak hills,
  Wherein thy nest is made.

I hear the wild bee's mellow chord,
　In airs that swim above;
The lesser hermit tunes his flute
　To solitude and love.

But thou, sweet singer of the wild,
　I give more heed to thee;
Thy wistful note of fond regret
　Strikes deeper chords in me.

Farewell, dear bird! I turn my face
　To other skies than thine —
A thousand leagues of land and sea
　Between thy home and mine.

TO THE LAPLAND LONGSPUR

By John Burroughs

I

OH, thou northland bobolink,
　　Looking over Summer's brink
Up to Winter, worn and dim,
Peering down from mountain
　　rim,
Something takes me in thy tone,
Quivering wing, and bubbling
　　throat;
Something moves me in thy ways —
Bird, rejoicing in thy days,
In thy upward-hovering flight.
In thy suit of black and white,

Chestnut cape and circled crown,
In thy mate of speckled brown;
Surely I may pause and think
Of my boyhood's bobolink.

II

Soaring over meadows wild
(Greener pastures never smiled);
Raining music from above,
Full of rapture, full of love;
Frolic, gay and debonair,
Yet not all exempt from care,
For thy nest is in the grass,
And thou worriest as I pass:
But nor hand nor foot of mine
Shall do harm to thee or thine;
I, musing, only pause to think
Of my boyhood's bobolink.

III

But no bobolink of mine
Ever sang o'er mead so fine,
Starred with flowers of every hue,
Gold and purple, white and blue;
Painted-cup, anemone,
Jacob's-ladder, fleur-de-lis,
Orchid, harebell, shooting-star,
Crane's-bill, lupine, seen afar,
Primrose, poppy, saxifrage,
Pictured type on Nature's page —

These and others here unnamed,
In northland gardens, yet untamed,
Deck the fields where thou dost sing,
Mounting up on trembling wing;
While in wistful mood I think
Of my boyhood's bobolink.

IV

On Unalaska's emerald lea,
On lonely isles in Bering Sea,
On far Siberia's barren shore,
On north Alaska's tundra floor,
At morn, at noon, in pallid night,
We heard thy song and saw thy flight,
While I, sighing, could but think
Of my boyhood's bobolink.

UNALASKA, July 18, 1899

THE CUP

By John Townsend Trowbridge

THE cup I sing is a cup of gold,
Many and many a century old,
Sculptured fair, and over-filled
With wine of a generous vintage, spilled
In crystal currents and foaming tides
All round its luminous, pictured sides.

Old Time enamelled and embossed
This ancient cup at an infinite cost.
Its frame he wrought of metal that run
Red from the furnace of the sun.
Ages on ages slowly rolled
Before the glowing mass was cold,
And still he toiled at the antique mould, —
Turning it fast in his fashioning hand,
Tracing circle, layer, and band,
Carving figures quaint and strange,
Pursuing, through many a wondrous change,
The symmetry of a plan divine.
At last he poured the lustrous wine,
Crowned high the radiant wave with light,
And held aloft the goblet bright,
Half in shadow, and wreathed in mist
Of purple, amber, and amethyst.

This is the goblet from whose brink
All creatures that have life must drink:
Foemen and lovers, haughty lord,
And sallow beggar with lips abhorred.
The new-born infant, ere it gain
The mother's breast, this wine must drain.
The oak with its subtile juice is fed,
The rose drinks till her cheeks are red,
And the dimpled, dainty violet sips
The limpid stream with loving lips.
It holds the blood of sun and star,
And all pure essences that are:
No fruit so high on the heavenly vine,
Whose golden hanging clusters shine

On the far-off shadowy midnight hills,
But some sweet influence it distils
That slideth down the silvery rills.
Here Wisdom drowned her dangerous thought,
The early gods their secrets brought;
Beauty, in quivering lines of light,
Ripples before the ravished sight;
And the unseen mystic spheres combine
To charm the cup and drug the wine.

All day I drink of the wine, and deep
In its stainless waves my senses steep;
All night my peaceful soul lies drowned
In hollows of the cup profound;
Again each morn I clamber up
The emerald crater of the cup,
On massive knobs of jasper stand
And view the azure ring expand:
I watch the foam-wreaths toss and swim
In the wine that o'erruns the jewelled rim:—
Edges of chrysolite emerge,
Dawn-tinted, from the misty surge:
My thrilled, uncovered front I lave,
My eager senses kiss the wave,
And drain, with its viewless draught, the lore
That kindles the bosom's secret core,
And the fire that maddens the poet's brain
With wild sweet ardor and heavenly pain.

TROUTING

By John Townsend Trowbridge

ITH slender rod, and line, and
    reel,
And feather-fly with sting of
    steel,
Whipping the brooks down sun-
    lit glades,
Wading the streams in woodland
    shades,
I come to the trouter's paradise :
The flashing fins leap twice or thrice :
Then idle on this gray bowlder lie
My crinkled line and colored fly,
While in the foam-flecked, glossy pool
The shy trout lurk secure and cool.

A rock-lined, wood-embosomed nook, —
Dim cloister of the chanting brook !
A chamber within the channelled hills,
Where the cold crystal brims and spills,
By dark-browed caverns blackly flows,
Falls from the cleft like crumbling snows,
And purls and plashes, breathing round
A soft, suffusing mist of sound.

Under a narrow belt of sky
Great bowlders in the torrent lie,
Huge stepping-stones where Titans cross !
Quaint broideries of vines and moss,

Of every loveliest hue and shape,
With tangle and braid and tassel drape
The beetling rocks, and veil the ledge,
And trail long fringe from the cataract's edge.
A hundred rills of nectar drip
From that Olympian beard and lip!

And, see! far on, it seems as if
In every crevice along the cliff
Some wild plant grew: the eye discerns
An ivied castle: feathery ferns
Nod from the frieze, and tuft the tall
Dismantled turret and ruined wall.

Strange gusts from deeper solitudes
Waft pungent odors of the woods.
The small, bee-haunted basswood-blooms
Drop in the gorge their faint perfumes.
Here all the wildwood flowers encamp,
That love the dimness and the damp.

High overhead the blue day shines;
The glad breeze swings in the singing pines.
Somewhere aloft in the boughs is heard
The fine note of some warbling bird.
In the alders, dank with noonday dews,
A restless cat-bird darts and mews.

Dear world! let summer tourists range
Your great highways in quest of change,
Go seek Niagara and the sea, —
This little nook sufficeth me!

So wild, so fresh, so solitary, —
I muse in its green sanctuary,
And breathe into my inmost sense
A pure, sweet, thrilling influence,
A bliss even innocent sport would stain,
And dear old Walton's art profane.

Here, lying beneath this leaning tree,
On the soft bank, it seems to me,
The winds that visit this lonely glen
Should soothe the souls of sorrowing men, —
The waters over these ledges curled
Might cool the heart of a fevered world!

THE PEWEE

By John Townsend Trowbridge

 THE listening Dryads hushed the woods;
The boughs were thick, and thin and few
The golden ribbons fluttering through;
Their sun-embroidered, leafy hoods
The lindens lifted to the blue:
Only a little forest-brook
The farthest hem of silence shook:
When in the hollow shades I heard, —
Was it a spirit, or a bird?

Or, strayed from Eden, desolate,
Some Peri calling to her mate,
　　Whom nevermore her mate would cheer?
　　　　"Pe-ri! pe-ri! peer!"

Through rocky clefts the brooklet fell
　　With plashy pour, that scarce was sound,
　　But only quiet less profound,
A stillness fresh and audible:
　　A yellow leaflet to the ground
Whirled noiselessly: with wing of gloss
A hovering sunbeam brushed the moss,
And, wavering brightly over it,
Sat like a butterfly alit:
The owlet in his open door
Stared roundly: while the breezes bore
　　The plaint to far-off places drear, —
　　　　"Pe-ree! pe-ree! peer!"

To trace it in its green retreat
　　I sought among the boughs in vain;
　　And followed still the wandering strain,
So melancholy and so sweet
　　The dim-eyed violets yearned with pain.
'Twas now a sorrow in the air,
Some nymph's immortalized despair
Haunting the woods and waterfalls;
And now, at long, sad intervals,
Sitting unseen in dusky shade,
His plaintive pipe some fairy played,
　　With long-drawn cadence thin and clear, —
　　　　"Pe-wee! pe-wee! peer!"

Long-drawn and clear its closes were, —
   As if the hand of Music through
   The sombre robe of Silence drew
A thread of golden gossamer :
   So pure a flute the fairy blew.
Like beggared princes of the wood,
In silver rags the birches stood ;
The hemlocks, lordly counsellors,
Were dumb ; the sturdy servitors,
In beechen jackets patched and gray,
Seemed waiting spellbound all the day
   That low, entrancing note to hear, —
      " Pe-wee ! pe-wee ! peer ! "

I quit the search, and sat me down
   Beside the brook, irresolute,
   And watched a little bird in suit
Of sober olive, soft and brown,
   Perched in the maple-branches, mute :
With greenish gold its vest was fringed,
Its tiny cap was ebon-tinged,
With ivory pale its wings were barred,
And its dark eyes were tender-starred.
" Dear bird," I said, " what is thy name ? "
And thrice the mournful answer came,
   So faint and far, and yet so near, —
      " Pe-wee ! pe-wee ! peer ! "

For so I found my forest bird, —
   The pewee of the loneliest woods,
   Sole singer in these solitudes,
Which never robin's whistle stirred,
   Where never bluebird's plume intrudes.

Quick darting through the dewy morn,
The redstart trilled his twittering horn,
And vanished in thick boughs : at even,
Like liquid pearls fresh showered from heaven,
The high notes of the lone wood-thrush
Fall on the forest's holy hush :
    But thou all day complainest here, —
        " Pe-wee ! pe-wee ! peer ! "

Hast thou, too, in thy little breast,
    Strange longings for a happier lot, —
    For love, for life, thou know'st not what, —
A yearning, and a vague unrest,
    For something still which thou hast not ? —
Thou soul of some benighted child
That perished, crying in the wild !
Or lost, forlorn, and wandering maid,
By love allured, by love betrayed,
Whose spirit with her latest sigh
Arose, a little wingèd cry,
    Above her chill and mossy bier !
        " Dear me ! dear me ! dear ! "

Ah, no such piercing sorrow mars
    The pewee's life of cheerful ease !
    He sings, or leaves his song to seize
An insect sporting in the bars
    Of mild bright light that gild the trees :
    A very poet he ! For him
All pleasant places still and dim :
His heart, a spark of heavenly fire,
Burns with undying, sweet desire :

And so he sings ; and so his song,
Though heard not by the hurrying throng,
   Is solace to the pensive ear :
      " Pewee ! pewee ! peer ! "

TO THE DANDELION

By James Russell Lowell

D EAR common flower, that
    grow'st beside the way,
Fringing the dusty road with
    harmless gold,
First pledge of blithesome May,
Which children pluck, and, full
    of pride uphold,
High-hearted buccaneers, o'erjoyed that they
An Eldorado in the grass have found,
Which not the rich earth's ample round
May match in wealth, thou art more dear to me
Than all the prouder summer-blooms may be.

  Gold such as thine ne'er drew the Spanish prow
Through the primeval hush of Indian seas,
   Nor wrinkled the lean brow
Of age, to rob the lover's heart of ease ;
   'Tis the Spring's largess, which she scatters now
To rich and poor alike, with lavish hand,
Though most hearts never understand
To take it at God's value, but pass by
The offered wealth with unrewarded eye.

Thou art my tropics and mine Italy;
To look at thee unlocks a warmer clime;
   The eyes thou givest me
Are in the heart, and heed not space or time:
   Not in mid June the golden-cuirassed bee
Feels a more summer-like warm ravishment
In the white lily's breezy tent,
His fragrant Sybaris, than I, when first
From the dark green thy yellow circles burst.

   Then think I of deep shadows on the grass,
Of meadows where in sun the cattle graze,
   Where, as the breezes pass,
The gleaming rushes lean a thousand ways,
   Of leaves that slumber in a cloudy mass,
Or whiten in the wind, of waters blue
That from the distance sparkle through
Some woodland gap, and of a sky above,
Where one white cloud like a stray lamb doth
    move.

   My childhood's earliest thoughts are linked with
    thee;
The sight of thee calls back the robin's song,
   Who, from the dark old tree
Beside the door, sang clearly all day long,
   And I, secure in childish piety,
Listened as if I heard an angel sing
With news from heaven, which he could bring
Fresh every day to my untainted ears
When birds and flowers and I were happy
    peers.

How like a prodigal doth nature seem,
When thou, for all thy gold, so common art!
    Thou teachest me to deem
More sacredly of every human heart,
    Since each reflects in joy its scanty gleam
Of heaven, and could some wondrous secret show,
Did we but pay the love we owe,
And with a child's undoubting wisdom look
On all these living pages of God's book.

THE BIGLOW PAPERS

No. 6

By James Russell Lowell

, COUNTRY-BORN an' bred,
        know where to find
    Some blooms thet make the sea-
        son suit the mind,
    An' seem to metch the doubtin'
        bluebird's notes, —
    Half-vent'rin' liverworts in furry
        coats,
Bloodroots, whose rolled-up leaves ef you oncurl,
Each on 'em's cradle to a baby-pearl, —
But these are jes' Spring's pickets; sure ez sin,
The rebble frosts 'll try to drive 'em in;
For half our May's so awfully like May n't,
'Twould rile a Shaker or an evrige saint;
Though I own up I like our back'ard springs
Thet kind o' haggle with their greens an' things,

An' when you 'mos give up, 'ithout more words
Toss the fields full o' blossoms, leaves, an' birds:
Thet's Northun natur' slow an' apt to doubt,
But when it *does* git stirred, ther' 's no gin-out !

Fust come the blackbirds clatt'rin' in tall trees,
An' settlin' things in windy Congresses, —
Queer politicians, though, for I'll be skinned
Ef all on 'em don't head aginst the wind.
'Fore long the trees begin to show belief, —
The maple crimsons to a coral-reef,
Then saffern swarms swing off from all the willers
So plump they look like yaller caterpillars,
Then gray hossches'nuts leetle hands unfold
Softer'n a baby's be at three days old:
Thet's robin-redbreast's almanick ; he knows
Thet arter this ther's only blossom-snows;
So, choosin' out a handy crotch an' spouse,
He goes to plast'rin' his adobë house.

Then seems to come a hitch, — things lag behind,
Till some fine mornin' Spring makes up her mind,
An' ez, when snow-swelled rivers cresh their dams
Heaped-up with ice thet dovetails in an' jams,
A leak comes spirtin' thru some pin-hole cleft,
Grows stronger, fercer, tears out right an' left,
Then all the waters bow themselves an' come,
Suddin, in one gret slope o' shedderin' foam,
Jes' so our Spring gits everythin' in tune
An' gives one leap from April into June :
Then all comes crowdin' in ; afore you think,
Young oak-leaves mist the side-hill woods with pink;

The catbird in the laylock-bush is loud;
The orchards turn to heaps o' rosy cloud;
Red-cedars blossom tu, though few folks know it,
An' look all dipt in sunshine like a poet;
The lime-trees pile their solid stacks o' shade
An' drows'ly simmer with the bees' sweet trade;
In ellum-shrouds the flashin' hangbird clings
An' for the summer vy'ge his hammock slings;
All down the loose-walled lanes in archin' bowers
The barb'ry droops its strings o' golden flowers,
Whose shrinkin' hearts the school-gals love to try
With pins,—they'll worry yourn so, boys, bimeby!
But I don't love your cat'logue style,—do you?—
Ez ef to sell off Natur' by vendoo;
One word with blood in 't's twice ez good ez two:
'Nuff sed, June's bridesman, poet o' the year,
Gladness on wings, the bobolink, is here;
Half-hid in tip-top apple-blooms he swings,
Or climbs aginst the breeze with quiverin' wings,
Or, givin' way to 't in a mock despair,
Runs down, a brook o' laughter, thru the air.

DAYBREAK

By Henry Wadsworth Longfellow

A WIND came up out of the sea,
And said, "O mists, make room for
me."

It hailed the ships, and cried, "Sail on,
Ye mariners, the night is gone."

And hurried landward far away,
Crying, "Awake! it is the day."

It said unto the forest, "Shout!
Hang all your leafy banners out!"

It touched the wood-bird's folded wing,
And said, "O bird, awake and sing."

And o'er the farms, "O chanticleer,
Your clarion blow; the day is near."

It whispered to the fields of corn,
"Bow down, and hail the coming morn."

It shouted through the belfry-tower,
"Awake, O bell! proclaim the hour."

It crossed the churchyard with a sigh,
And said, "Not yet! in quiet lie."

RAIN IN SUMMER

By Henry Wadsworth Longfellow

HOW beautiful is the rain!
After the dust and heat,
In the broad and fiery street,
In the narrow lane,
How beautiful is the rain!

How it clatters along the roofs,
Like the tramp of hoofs!
How it gushes and struggles out
From the throat of the overflowing spout!

Across the window pane
It pours and pours;
And swift and wide,
With a muddy tide,
Like a river down the gutter roars
The rain, the welcome rain!

The sick man from his chamber looks
At the twisted brooks;
He can feel the cool
Breath of each little pool;
His fevered brain
Grows calm again,
And he breathes a blessing on the rain

From the neighboring school
Come the boys,
With more than their wonted noise
And commotion;
And down the wet streets
Sail their mimic fleets,
Till the treacherous pool
Ingulfs them in its whirling
And turbulent ocean.

In the country, on every side,
Where far and wide,
Like a leopard's tawny and spotted hide,
Stretches the plain,
To the dry grass and the drier grain
How welcome is the rain!

In the furrowed land
The toilsome and patient oxen stand;
Lifting the yoke-encumbered head,
With their dilated nostrils spread,
They silently inhale
The clover-scented gale,
And the vapors that arise
From the well-watered and smoking soil.
For this rest in the furrow after toil
Their large and lustrous eyes
Seem to thank the Lord,
More than man's spoken word.

Near at hand,
From under the sheltering trees,
The farmer sees
His pastures, and his fields of grain,
As they bend their tops
To the numberless beating drops
Of the incessant rain.
He counts it as no sin
That he sees therein
Only his own thrift and gain.

These, and far more than these,
The Poet sees!
He can behold
Aquarius old
Walking the fenceless fields of air;
And from each ample fold
Of the clouds about him rolled
Scattering everywhere

The showery rain,
As the farmer scatters his grain.

He can behold
Things manifold
That have not yet been wholly told, —
Have not been wholly sung nor said.
For his thought, that never stops,
Follows the water-drops
Down to the graves of the dead,
Down through chasms and gulfs profound,
To the dreary fountain-head
Of lakes and rivers under ground ;
And sees them, when the rain is done,
On the bridge of colors seven
Climbing up once more to heaven,
Opposite the setting sun.

Thus the Seer,
With vision clear,
Sees forms appear and disappear,
In the perpetual round of strange
Mysterious change
From birth to death, from death to birth,
From earth to heaven, from heaven to earth ;
Till glimpses more sublime
Of things, unseen before,
Unto his wondering eyes reveal
The Universe, as an immeasurable wheel
Turning forevermore
In the rapid and rushing river of Time.

THE BRIDGE

By Henry Wadsworth Longfellow

I STOOD on the bridge at mid-
  night,
  As the clocks were striking
    the hour,
And the moon rose o'er the city,
  Behind the dark church-
    tower.

I saw her bright reflection
  In the waters under me,
Like a golden goblet falling
  And sinking into the sea.

And far in the hazy distance
  Of that lovely night in June,
The blaze of the flaming furnace
  Gleamed redder than the moon.

Among the long, black rafters
  The wavering shadows lay,
And the current that came from the ocean
  Seemed to lift and bear them away,

As, sweeping and eddying through them,
  Rose the belated tide,
And, streaming into the moonlight,
  The seaweed floated wide.

And like those waters rushing
    Among the wooden piers
A flood of thoughts came o'er me
    That filled my eyes with tears.

How often, O how often,
    In the days that had gone by,
I had stood on that bridge at midnight,
    And gazed on that wave and sky!

How often, O how often,
    I had wished that the ebbing tide
Would bear me away on its bosom
    O'er the ocean wild and wide!

For my heart was hot and restless,
    And my life was full of care,
And the burden laid upon me
    Seemed greater than I could bear.

But now it has fallen from me,
    It is buried in the sea;
And only the sorrow of others
    Throws its shadow over me.

Yet whenever I cross the river
    On its bridge with wooden piers,
Like the odor of brine from the ocean
    Comes the thought of other years.

And I think how many thousands
    Of care-encumbered men,
Each bearing his burden of sorrow,
    Have crossed the bridge since then.

I see the long procession
  Still passing to and fro,
The young heart hot and restless,
  And the old subdued and slow!

And for ever and for ever
  As long as the river flows,
As long as the heart has passions,
  As long as life has woes;

The moon and its broken reflection
  And its shadows shall appear,
As the symbol of love in heaven,
  And its wavering image here.

MY AVIARY

By Oliver Wendell Holmes

THROUGH my north window,
    in the wintry weather, —
    My airy oriel on the river
      shore, —
I watch the sea-fowl as they flock
    together
  Where late the boatman flashed
    his dripping oar.

The gull, high floating, like a sloop unladen,
  Lets the loose water waft him as it will;
The duck, round-breasted as a rustic maiden,
  Paddles and plunges, busy, busy still.

I see the solemn gulls in council sitting
  On some broad ice-floe, pondering long and late,
While overhead the home-bound ducks are flitting,
  And leave the tardy conclave in debate,

Those weighty questions in their breasts revolving
  Whose deeper meaning science never learns,
Till at some reverend elder's look dissolving,
  The speechless senate silently adjourns.

But when along the waves the shrill north-easter
  Shrieks through the laboring coaster's shrouds
    " Beware ! "
The pale bird, kindling like a Christmas feaster
  When some wild chorus shakes the vinous air,

Flaps from the leaden wave in fierce rejoicing,
  Feels heaven's dumb lightning thrill his torpid
    nerves,
Now on the blast his whistling plumage poising,
  Now wheeling, whirling in fantastic curves.

Such is our gull ; a gentleman of leisure,
  Less fleshed than feathered ; bagged you'll find
    him such ;
His virtue silence ; his employment pleasure ;
  Not bad to look at, and not good for much.

What of our duck ? He has some highbred
    cousins, —
  His Grace the Canvas-back, My Lord the
    Brant, —
Anas and *Anser* — both served up by dozens,
  At Boston's *Rocher*, half-way to Nahant.

As for himself, he seems alert and thriving,
   Grubs up a living somehow — what, who knows ?
Crabs ? mussels ? weeds ? — Look quick ! there's
   one just diving !
    Flop ! Splash ! his white breast glistens — down
    he goes !

And while he's under — just about a minute —
   I take advantage of the fact to say
His fishy carcase has no virtue in it
   The gunning idiot's worthless hire to pay.

He knows you ! " sportsmen " from suburban
   alleys,
   Stretched under seaweed in the treacherous
   punt ;
Knows every lazy, shiftless lout that sallies
   Forth to waste powder — as *he* says, to " hunt."

I watch you with a patient satisfaction,
   Well pleased to discount your predestined luck ;
The float that figures in your sly transaction
   Will carry back a goose, but not a duck.

Shrewd is our bird ; not easy to outwit him !
   Sharp is the outlook of those pin-head eyes ;
Still, he is mortal and a shot may hit him,
   One cannot always miss him if he tries.

Look ! there's a young one, dreaming not of
   danger ;
   Sees a flat log come floating down the stream ;
Stares undismayed upon the harmless stranger ;
   Ah ! were all strangers harmless as they seem !

Habet! a leaden shower his breast has shattered ;
  Vainly he flutters, not again to rise ;
His soft white plumes along the waves are scattered ;
  Helpless the wing that braved the tempest lies.

He sees his comrades high above him flying
  To seek their nests among the island reeds ;
Strong is their flight ; all lonely he is lying
  Washed by the crimsoned water as he bleeds.

O Thou who carest for the falling sparrow,
  Canst Thou the sinless sufferer's pang forget ?
Or is Thy dread account-book's page so narrow
  Its one long column scores Thy creatures' debt ?

Poor gentle guest, by nature kindly cherished,
  A world grows dark with thee in blinding death ;
One little gasp — thy universe has perished,
  Wrecked by the idle thief who stole thy breath !

Is this the whole sad story of creation,
  Lived by its breathing myriads o'er and o'er, —
One glimpse of day, then black annihilation, —
  A sunlit passage to a sunless shore ?

Give back our faith, ye mystery-solving lynxes !
  Robe us once more in heaven-aspiring creeds !
Happier was dreaming Egypt with her sphynxes,
  The stony convent with its cross and beads !

How often gazing where a bird reposes,
  Rocked on the wavelets, drifting with the tide,
I lose myself in strange metempsychosis
  And float a sea-fowl at a sea-fowl's side.

From rain, hail, snow in feathery mantle muffled,
  Clear-eyed, strong-limbed, with keenest sense to
    hear
My mate soft murmuring, who, with plumes un-
    ruffled,
  Where'er I wander still is nestling near;

The great blue hollow like a garment o'er me;
  Space all unmeasured, unrecorded time;
While seen with inward eye moves on before me
  Thought's pictured train in wordless pantomime.

A voice recalls me.   From my window turning
  I find myself a plumeless biped still;
No beak, no claws, no sign of wings discerning, —
  In fact with nothing bird-like but my quill.

MIDSUMMER

By Oliver Wendell Holmes

ERE! sweep these foolish leaves away,
  I will not crush my brains to-
    day!
Look! are the southern curtains
    drawn?
Fetch me a fan, and so begone!

Not that, the palm-tree's rustling leaf
Brought from a parching coral-reef!
Its breath is heated; — I would swing
The broad gray plumes, — the eagle's wing.

I hate these roses' feverish blood! —
Pluck me a half-blown lily-bud,

A long-stemmed lily from the lake,
Cold as a coiling water-snake.

Rain me sweet odors on the air,
And wheel me up my Indian chair,
And spread some book not overwise
Flat out before my sleepy eyes.

— Who knows it not, — this dead recoil
Of weary fibres stretched with toil, —
The pulse that flutters faint and low
When Summer's seething breezes blow!

O Nature! bare thy loving breast,
And give thy child one hour of rest, —
One little hour to lie unseen
Beneath thy scarf of leafy green!

So, curtained by a singing pine,
Its murmuring voice shall blend with mine,
Till, lost in dreams, my faltering lay
In sweeter music dies away.

TO AN INSECT

By Oliver Wendell Holmes.

I LOVE to hear thine earnest voice,
　　Wherever thou art hid,
　　Thou testy little dogmatist,
　Thou pretty Katydid!
Thou mindest me of gentlefolks, —
　Old gentlefolks are they, —
Thou say'st an undisputed thing
　In such a solemn way.

Thou art a female, Katydid!
  I know it by the trill
That quivers through thy piercing notes,
  So petulant and shrill;
I think there is a knot of you
  Beneath the hollow tree, —
A knot of spinster Katydids, —
  Do Katydids drink tea?

O tell me where did Katy live,
  And what did Katy do?
And was she very fair and young,
  And yet so wicked, too?
Did Katy love a naughty man,
  Or kiss more cheeks than one?
I warrant Katy did no more
  Than many a Kate has done.

Dear me! I'll tell you all about
  My fuss with little Jane,
And Ann, with whom I used to walk
  So often down the lane,
And all that tore their locks of black,
  Or wet their eyes of blue, —
Pray tell me, sweetest Katydid,
  What did poor Katy do?

Ah no! the living oak shall crash,
  That stood for ages still,
The rock shall rend its mossy base
  And thunder down the hill,

Before the little Katydid
　Shall add one word, to tell
The mystic story of the maid
　Whose name she knows so well.

Peace to the ever-murmuring race !
　And when the latest one
Shall fold in death her feeble wings
　Beneath the autumn sun,
Then shall she raise her fainting voice,
　And lift her drooping lid,
And then the child of future years
　Shall hear what Katy did.

THE PLANTING OF THE APPLE-TREE

By *William Cullen Bryant*

COME, let us plant the apple-tree.
　Cleave the tough greensward
　　with the spade ;
Wide let its hollow bed be made ;
There gently lay the roots, and
　　there
Sift the dark mould with kindly care,
　And press it o'er them tenderly,
As, round the sleeping infant's feet,
We softly fold the cradle-sheet ;
　So plant we the apple-tree.

What plant we in this apple-tree?
Buds, which the breath of summer days
Shall lengthen into leafy sprays;
Boughs where the thrush, with crimson breast,
Shall haunt and sing and hide her nest;
　We plant, upon the sunny lea,
A shadow for the noontide hour,
A shelter from the summer shower,
　When we plant the apple-tree.

What plant we in this apple-tree?
Sweets for a hundred flowery springs
To load the May-wind's restless wings,
When, from the orchard-row, he pours
Its fragrance through our open doors;
　A world of blossoms for the bee,
Flowers for the sick girl's silent room,
For the glad infant sprigs of bloom,
　We plant with the apple-tree.

What plant we in this apple-tree?
Fruits that shall swell in sunny June,
And redden in the August noon,
And drop, when gentle airs come by,
That fan the blue September sky,
　While children come, with cries of glee,
And seek them where the fragrant grass
Betrays their bed to those who pass,
　At the foot of the apple-tree.

And when, above this apple-tree,
The winter stars are quivering bright,
And winds go howling through the night,

Girls, whose young eyes o'erflow with mirth,
Shall peel its fruit by cottage-hearth,
    And guests in prouder homes shall see,
Heaped with the grape of Cintra's vine
And golden orange of the line,
    The fruit of the apple-tree.

The fruitage of this apple-tree
Winds and our flag of stripe and star
Shall bear to coasts that lie afar,
Where men shall wonder at the view,
And ask in what fair groves they grew;
    And sojourners beyond the sea
Shall think of childhood's careless day,
And long, long hours of summer play,
    In the shade of the apple-tree.

Each year shall give this apple-tree
A broader flush of roseate bloom,
A deeper maze of verdurous gloom,
And loosen, when the frost-clouds lower,
The crisp brown leaves in thicker shower.
    The years shall come and pass, but we
Shall hear no longer, where we lie,
The summer's songs, the autumn's sigh,
    In the boughs of the apple-tree.

And time shall waste this apple-tree.
Oh, when its aged branches throw
Thin shadows on the ground below,
Shall fraud and force and iron will
Oppress the weak and helpless still?

What shall the tasks of mercy be,
Amid the toils, the strifes, the tears
Of those who live when length of years
    Is wasting this little apple-tree?

"Who planted this old apple-tree?"
The children of that distant day
Thus to some aged man shall say;
And, gazing on its mossy stem,
The gray-haired man shall answer them:
    "A poet of the land was he,
Born in the rude but good old times;
'Tis said he made some quaint old rhymes,
    On planting the apple-tree."

THE PATH

By *William Cullen Bryant*

THE path we planned beneath
    October's sky,
    Along the hillside, through the
        woodland shade,
Is finished; thanks to thee, whose
        kindly eye
    Has watched me, as I plied
        the busy spade;
Else had I wearied, ere this path of ours
Had pierced the woodland to its inner bowers.

Yet, 'twas a pleasant toil to trace and beat,
    Among the glowing trees, this winding way,
While the sweet autumn sunshine, doubly sweet,
    Flushed with the ruddy foliage, round us lay,

As if some gorgeous cloud of morning stood,
In glory, mid the arches of the wood.

A path ! what beauty does a path bestow
   Even on the dreariest wild ! its savage nooks
Seem homelike where accustomed footsteps go,
   And the grim rock puts on familiar looks.
The tangled swamp, through which a pathway
     strays,
Becomes a garden with strange flowers and sprays.

See from the weedy earth a rivulet break
   And purl along the untrodden wilderness ;
There the shy cuckoo comes his thirst to slake,
   There the shrill jay alights his plumes to dress ;
And there the stealthy fox, when morn is gray,
Laps the clear stream and lightly moves away.

But let a path approach that fountain's brink,
   And nobler forms of life, behold ! are there :
Boys kneeling with protruded lips to drink,
   And slender maids that homeward slowly bear
The brimming pail, and busy dames that lay
Their webs to whiten in the summer ray.

Then know we that for herd and flock are poured
   Those pleasant streams that o'er the pebbles
     slip ;
Those pure sweet waters sparkle on the board ;
   Those fresh cool waters wet the sick man's lip ;
Those clear bright waters from the font are shed,
In dews of baptism, on the infant's head.

What different steps the rural footway trace!
   The laborer afield at early day;
The schoolboy sauntering with uneven pace;
   The Sunday worshipper in fresh array;
And mourner in the weeds of sorrow drest;
And, smiling to himself, the wedding guest.

There he who cons a speech and he who hums
   His yet unfinished verses, musing walk.
There, with her little brood, the matron comes,
   To break the spring flower from its juicy stalk;
And lovers, loitering, wonder that the moon
Has risen upon their pleasant stroll so soon.

Bewildered in vast woods, the traveller feels
   His heavy heart grow lighter, if he meet
The traces of a path, and straight he kneels,
   And kisses the dear print of human feet,
And thanks his God, and journeys without fear,
For now he knows the abodes of men are near.

Pursue the slenderest path across the lawn;
   Lo! on the broad highway it issues forth,
And, blended with the greater track, goes on,
   Over the surface of the mighty earth,
Climbs hills and crosses vales, and stretches far,
Through silent forests, toward the evening star —

And enters cities murmuring with the feet
   Of multitudes, and wanders forth again,
And joins the climes of frost to climes of heat,
   Binds East to West, and marries main to main,
Nor stays till at the long-resounding shore
Of the great deep, where paths are known no more.

Oh, mighty instinct, that dost thus unite
 Earth's neighborhoods and tribes with friendly
  bands,
What guilt is theirs who, in their greed or spite,
 Undo thy holy work with violent hands,
And post their squadrons, nursed in war's grim
  trade,
To bar the ways for mutual succor made!

JUNE

By William Cullen Bryant

GAZED upon the glorious sky
  And the green mountains
   round,
And thought that when I came
  to lie
 At rest within the ground,
'Twere pleasant, that in flowery
  June,
When brooks send up a cheerful tune,
 And groves a joyous sound,
The sexton's hand, my grave to make,
The rich, green mountain-turf should break.

A cell within the frozen mould,
 A coffin borne through sleet,
And icy clods above it rolled,
 While fierce the tempests beat —
Away! — I will not think of these —
Blue be the sky and soft the breeze,
 Earth green beneath the feet,

And be the damp mould gently pressed
Into my narrow place of rest.

There through the long, long summer hours,
   The golden light should lie,
And thick young herbs and groups of flowers
   Stand in their beauty by.
The oriole should build and tell
His love-tale close beside my cell;
   The idle butterfly
Should rest him there, and there be heard
The housewife bee and humming-bird.

And what if cheerful shouts at noon
   Come from the village sent,
Or songs of maids, beneath the moon
   With fairy laughter blent?
And what if, in the evening light,
Betrothèd lovers walk in sight
   Of my low monument?
I would the lovely scene around
Might know no sadder sight nor sound.

I know that I no more should see
   The season's glorious show,
Nor would its brightness shine for me,
   Nor its wild music flow;
But if, around my place of sleep,
The friends I love should come to weep,
   They might not haste to go.
Soft airs, and song, and light, and bloom
Should keep them lingering by my tomb.

These to their softened hearts should bear
   The thought of what has been,
And speak of one who cannot share
   The gladness of the scene;
Whose part, in all the pomp that fills
The circuit of the summer hills,
   Is that his grave is green;
And deeply would their hearts rejoice
To hear again his living voice.

TO A WATERFOWL

By *William Cullen Bryant*

HITHER, midst falling dew,
   While glow the heavens with
     the last steps of day,
Far, through their rosy depths,
    dost thou pursue
     Thy solitary way?

Vainly the fowler's eye
   Might mark thy distant flight to do thee wrong,
As, darkly painted on the crimson sky,
   Thy figure floats along.

Seek'st thou the plashy brink
   Of weedy lake, or marge of river wide,
Or where the rocking billows rise and sink
   On the chafed ocean-side?

There is a Power whose care
  Teaches thy way along that pathless coast, —
The desert and illimitable air —
  Lone wandering, but not lost.

All day thy wings have fanned,
  At that far height the cold, thin atmosphere,
Yet stoop not, weary, to the welcome land,
  Though the dark night is near.

And soon that toil shall end ;
  Soon shalt thou find a summer home, and rest,
And scream among thy fellows: reeds shall bend,
  Soon, o'er thy sheltered nest.

Thou'rt gone, the abyss of heaven
  Hath swallowed up thy form ; yet, on my heart
Deeply has sunk the lesson thou hast given,
  And shall not soon depart.

He who, from zone to zone,
  Guides through the boundless sky thy certain
    flight,
In the long way that I must tread alone,
  Will lead my steps aright.

AN INVITATION TO THE COUNTRY

By *William Cullen Bryant*

LREADY, close by our summer
dwelling,
  The Easter sparrow repeats
  her song;
A merry warbler, she chides the
  blossoms —
  The idle blossoms that sleep
  so long.

The bluebird chants, from the elm's long branches,
  A hymn to welcome the budding year.
The south wind wanders from field to forest,
  And softly whispers, " The Spring is here."

Come, daughter mine, from the gloomy city,
  Before those lays from the elm have ceased;
The violet breathes, by our door, as sweetly
  As in the air of her native East.

Though many a flower in the wood is waking,
  The daffodil is our doorside queen;
She pushes upward the sward already,
  To spot with sunshine the early green.

No lays so joyous as these are warbled
  From wiry prison in maiden's bower;
No pampered bloom of the green-house chamber
  Has half the charm of the lawn's first flower.

Yet these sweet sounds of the early season,
  And these fair sights of its sunny days,
Are only sweet when we fondly listen,
  And only fair when we fondly gaze.

There is no glory in star or blossom
  Till looked upon by a loving eye;
There is no fragrance in April breezes
  Till breathed with joy as they wander by.

Come, Julia dear, for the sprouting willows,
  The opening flowers, and the gleaming brooks,
And hollows, green in the sun, are waiting
  Their dower of beauty from thy glad looks.

THE GLADNESS OF NATURE

By *William Cullen Bryant*

 IS this a time to be cloudy and sad,
    When our mother Nature
      laughs around;
  When even the deep blue heav-
    ens look glad,
    And gladness breathes from
      the blossoming ground?

There are notes of joy from the hang-bird and wren
  And the gossip of swallows through all the sky;
The ground-squirrel gayly chirps by his den,
  And the wilding bee hums merrily by.

The clouds are at play in the azure space
   And their shadows at play on the bright-green
      vale,
And here they stretch to the frolic chase,
   And there they roll on the easy gale.

There's a dance of leaves in that aspen bower,
   There's a titter of winds in that beechen tree,
There's a smile on the fruit, and a smile on the
      flower,
   And a laugh from the brook that runs to the sea.

And look at the broad-faced sun, how he smiles
   On the dewy earth that smiles in his ray,
On the leaping waters and gay young isles;
   Ay, look, and he'll smile thy gloom away.

TO THE SMALL CELANDINE*

By William Wordsworth

PANSIES, lilies, kingcups, daisies,
   Let them live upon their praises;
   Long as there's a sun that sets,
   Primroses will have their glory;
   Long as there are violets,
   They will have a place in story:
   There's a flower that shall be
      mine,
'Tis the little Celandine.

Eyes of some men travel far
For the finding of a star;

          * Common Pilewort.

Up and down the heavens they go,
Men that keep a mighty rout!
I'm as great as they, I trow,
Since the day I found thee out,
Little Flower! — I'll make a stir,
Like a sage astronomer.

Modest, yet withal an Elf
Bold, and lavish of thyself;
Since we needs must first have met
I have seen thee, high and low,
Thirty years or more, and yet
'Twas a face I did not know;
Thou hast now, go where I may,
Fifty greetings in a day.

Ere a leaf is on a bush,
In the time before the thrush
Has a thought about her nest,
Thou wilt come with half a call,
Spreading out thy glossy breast
Like a careless Prodigal;
Telling tales about the sun,
When we've little warmth, or none.

Poets, vain men in their mood!
Travel with the multitude:
Never heed them; I aver
That they all are wanton wooers;
But the thrifty cottager,
Who stirs little out of doors,
Joys to spy thee near her home;
Spring is coming, Thou art come!

Comfort have thou of thy merit,
Kindly, unassuming Spirit!
Careless of thy neighborhood,
Thou dost show thy pleasant face
On the moor, and in the wood,
In the lane; — there's not a place,
Howsoever mean it be,
But 'tis good enough for thee.

Ill befall the yellow flowers,
Children of the flaring hours!
Buttercups, that will be seen,
Whether we will see or no;
Others, too, of lofty mien;
They have done as worldlings do,
Taken praise that should be thine,
Little, humble Celandine!

Prophet of delight and mirth,
Ill-requited upon earth;
Herald of a mighty band,
Of a joyous train ensuing,
Serving at my heart's command,
Tasks that are no tasks renewing,
I will sing, as doth behove,
Hymns in praise of what I love!

THREE YEARS SHE GREW IN SUN AND SHOWER

By *William Wordsworth*

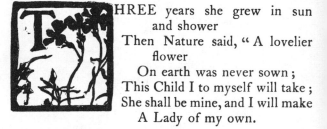

THREE years she grew in sun
    and shower
Then Nature said, " A lovelier
    flower
  On earth was never sown ;
This Child I to myself will take ;
She shall be mine, and I will make
  A Lady of my own.

" Myself will to my darling be
Both law and impulse : and with me
  The Girl, in rock and plain,
In earth and heaven, in glade and bower,
Shall feel an overseeing power
  To kindle or restrain.

" She shall be sportive as the fawn
That wild with glee across the lawn
  Or up the mountain springs ;
And hers shall be the breathing balm,
And hers the silence and the calm
  Of mute insensate things.

" The floating clouds their state shall lend
To her ; for her the willow bend ;

Nor shall she fail to see
Even in the motions of the Storm
Grace that shall mould the Maiden's form
By silent sympathy.

" The stars of midnight shall be dear
To her; and she shall lend her ear
In many a secret place
Where rivulets dance their wayward round,
And beauty born of murmuring sound
Shall pass into her face.

" And vital feelings of delight
Shall rear her form to stately height,
Her virgin bosom swell;
Such thoughts to Lucy I will give
While she and I together live
Here in this happy dell."

Thus Nature spake — The work was done —
How soon my Lucy's race was run!
She died, and left to me
This heath, this calm and quiet scene;
The memory of what has been,
And never more will be.

———

A slumber did my spirit seal,
    I had no human fears:
She seemed a thing that could not feel
    The touch of earthly years.

No motion has she now, no force;
  She neither hears nor sees;
Rolled round in earth's diurnal course
  With rocks, and stones, and trees!

THE NIGHTINGALE

By *William Wordsworth*

 NIGHTINGALE! thou surely art
A creature of a " fiery heart ": —
These notes of thine — they pierce and pierce;
Tumultuous harmony and fierce!
Thou sing'st as if the God of wine
Had helped thee to a Valentine;
A song in mockery and despite
Of shades, and dews, and silent night;
And steady bliss, and all the loves
Now sleeping in these peaceful groves.

I heard a Stock-dove sing or say
His homely tale, this very day;
His voice was buried among trees,
Yet to be come-at by the breeze:
He did not cease; but cooed — and cooed;
And somewhat pensively he wooed:
He sang of love with quiet blending,
Slow to begin, and never ending;
Of serious faith, and inward glee;
That was the song — the song for me!

TO A SKYLARK

By *William Wordsworth*

P with me! up with me into the
  clouds!
 For thy song, Lark, is strong;
Up with me, up with me into the
  clouds!
  Singing, singing,
With clouds and sky about thee
  ringing,
Lift me, guide me, till I find
That spot which seems so to thy mind!

I have walked through wildernesses dreary,
And to-day my heart is weary;
Had I now the wings of a Faery,
Up to thee would I fly.
There's madness about thee, and joy divine
In that song of thine;
Lift me, guide me, high and high
To thy banqueting-place in the sky.

  Joyous as morning,
Thou art laughing and scorning;
Thou hast a nest for thy love and thy rest,
And, though little troubled with sloth,
Drunken Lark! thou wouldst be loth
To be such a traveller as I.

Happy, happy Liver,
With a soul as strong as a mountain river,
Pouring out praise to the Almighty Giver,
　Joy and jollity be with us both!

　Alas! my journey, rugged and uneven,
Through prickly moors or dusty ways must wind;
But hearing thee, or others of thy kind,
As full of gladness and as free of heaven,
I, with my fate contented, will plod on,
And hope for higher raptures when life's day is
　　done.

TINTERN ABBEY

By William Wordsworth

 HAVE learned
To look on nature, not as in the
　hour
Of thoughtless youth, but hearing
　oftentimes
The still, sad music of humanity,
Not harsh nor grating, though of
　ample power
To chasten and subdue.　And I have felt
A presence that disturbs me with the joy
Of elevated thoughts; a sense sublime
Of something far more deeply interfused,
Whose dwelling is the light of setting suns,
And the round ocean and the living air,

And the blue sky, and in the mind of man :
A motion and a spirit, that impels
All thinking things, all objects of all thought,
And rolls through all things.   Therefore am I still
A lover of the meadows and the woods,
And mountains; and of all that we behold
From this green earth ; of all the mighty world
Of eye, and ear, — both what they half create,
And what perceive ; well pleased to recognize
In nature and the language of the sense
The anchor of my purest thoughts.

TO THE CUCKOO

By William Wordsworth

BLITHE New-comer !   I have heard,
I hear thee and rejoice.
O   Cuckoo ! shall I call thee Bird,
Or but a wandering Voice ?

While I am lying on the grass
Thy twofold shout I hear,
From hill to hill it seems to pass,
At once far off, and near.

Though babbling only to the Vale,
Of sunshine and of flowers,
Thou bringest unto me a tale
Of visionary hours.

Thrice welcome, darling of the Spring!
Even yet thou art to me
No Bird, but an invisible thing,
A voice, a mystery;

The same whom in my school-boy days
I listened to; that Cry
Which made me look a thousand ways
In bush, and tree, and sky.

To seek thee did I often rove
Through woods and on the green;
And thou wert still a hope, a love;
Still longed for, never seen.

And I can listen to thee yet;
Can lie upon the plain
And listen, till I do beget
That golden time again.

O blessed Bird! the earth we pace
Again appears to be
An unsubstantial, faery place,
That is fit home for Thee!

A NIGHT PIECE *

By William Wordsworth

The sky is overcast
With a continuous cloud of texture close,
Heavy and wan, all whitened by the Moon,
Which through that veil is indistinctly seen,
A dull, contracted circle, yielding light
So feebly spread, that not a shadow falls,
Chequering the ground — from rock, plant, tree, or
    tower.
At length a pleasant instantaneous gleam
Startles the pensive traveller while he treads
His lonesome path, with unobserving eye
Bent earthwards; he looks up — the clouds are
    split
Asunder, — and above his head he sees
The clear Moon, and the glory of the heavens.
There in a black-blue vault she sails along,
Followed by multitudes of stars, that, small
And sharp, and bright, along the dark abyss
Drive as she drives: how fast they wheel away,
Yet vanish not! — the wind is in the tree,
But they are silent; — still they roll along
Immeasurably distant; and the vault,
Built round by those white clouds, enormous
    clouds,
Still deepens its unfathomable depth.
At length the Vision closes; and the mind,

* The poetical works of William Wordsworth. Edited by E.
Dowden, 1892, Vol. 2, p. 88.

Not undisturbed by the delight it feels,
Which slowly settles into peaceful calm,
Is left to muse upon the solemn scene.

TO MY SISTER

By William Wordsworth

Written at a small distance from my house, and sent by
my little boy.

I T is the first mild day of March :
Each minute sweeter than be-
fore,
The redbreast sings from the
tall larch
That stands beside our door.

There is a blessing in the air,
Which seems a sense of joy to yield
To the bare trees, and mountains bare,
And grass in the green field.

My sister ! ('tis a wish of mine)
Now that our morning meal is done,
Make haste, your morning task resign ;
Come forth and feel the sun.

Edward will come with you ; — and, pray,
Put on with speed your woodland dress ;
And bring no book : for this one day
We'll give to idleness.

No joyless forms shall regulate
Our living calendar :
We from to-day, my Friend, will date
The opening of the year.

Love, now a universal birth,
From heart to heart is stealing,
From earth to man, from man to earth :
— It is the hour of feeling.

One moment now may give us more
Than years of toiling reason :
Our minds shall drink at every pore
The spirit of the season.

Some silent laws our hearts will make,
Which they shall long obey :
We for the year to come may take
Our temper from to-day.

And from the blessed power that rolls
About, below, above,
We'll frame the measure of our souls :
They shall be turned to love.

Then come, my Sister; come, I pray,
With speed put on your woodland dress ;
And bring no book : for this one day
We'll give to idleness.

LINES WRITTEN IN EARLY SPRING

By *William Wordsworth*

HEARD a thousand blended notes,
While in a grove I sate reclined,
In that sweet mood when pleasant thoughts
Bring sad thoughts to the mind.

To her fair works did Nature link
The human soul that through me ran;
And much it grieved my heart to think
What man has made of man.

Through primrose tufts, in that sweet bower,
The periwinkle trailed its wreaths;
And 'tis my faith that every flower
Enjoys the air it breathes.

The birds around me hopped and played;
Their thoughts I cannot measure:—
But the least motion which they made,
It seemed a thrill of pleasure.

The budding twigs spread out their fan,
To catch the breezy air;
And I must think, do all I can,
That there was pleasure there.

If this belief from heaven be sent,
If such be Nature's holy plan,
Have I not reason to lament
What man has made of man ?

THERE WAS A BOY

By William Wordsworth

THERE was a Boy; ye knew him
    well, ye cliffs
And islands of Winander ! —
    many a time,
At evening, when the earliest
    stars began
To move along the edges of the
    hills,
Rising or setting, would he stand alone,
Beneath the trees, or by the glimmering lake ;
And there, with fingers interwoven, both hands
Pressed closely palm to palm and to his mouth
Uplifted, he, as through an instrument,
Blew mimic hootings to the silent owls,
That they might answer him. — And they would
    shout
Across the watery vale, and shout again,
Responsive to his call, — with quivering peals,
And long halloos, and screams, and echoes loud
Redoubled and redoubled ; concourse wild
Of jocund din ! And, when there came a pause
Of silence such as baffled his best skill :

Then, sometimes, in that silence, while he hung
Listening, a gentle shock of mild surprise
Has carried far into his heart the voice
Of mountain torrents; or the visible scene
Would enter unawares into his mind
With all its solemn imagery, its rocks,
Its woods, and that uncertain heaven received
Into the bosom of the steady lake.

This boy was taken from his mates, and died
In childhood, ere he was full twelve years old.
Pre-eminent in beauty is the vale
Where he was born and bred : the church-yard
   hangs
Upon a slope above the village school;
And, through that church-yard when my way has
   led
On summer evenings, I believe that there
A long half-hour together I have stood
Mute — looking at the grave in which he lies !

"UP! UP! MY FRIEND, AND QUIT YOUR BOOKS"

By William Wordsworth

UP! up! my Friend, and quit your books;
   Or surely you'll grow double :
    Up! up! my Friend, and clear your looks;
Why all this toil and trouble?

The sun, above the mountain's head,
A freshening lustre mellow
Through all the long green fields has spread,
His first sweet evening yellow.

Books! 'tis a dull and endless strife :
Come, hear the woodland linnet,
How sweet his music! on my life,
There's more of wisdom in it.

And hark! how blithe the throstle sings!
He, too, is no mean preacher :
Come forth into the light of things,
Let Nature be your Teacher.

She has a world of ready wealth,
Our minds and hearts to bless —
Spontaneous wisdom breathed by health,
Truth breathed by cheerfulness.

One impulse from a vernal wood
May teach you more of man,
Of moral evil and of good,
Than all the sages can.

Sweet is the lore which Nature brings;
Our meddling intellect
Misshapes the beauteous forms of things : —
We murder to dissect.

Enough of Science and of Art;
Close up these barren leaves;
Come forth, and bring with you a heart
That watches and receives.

DAFFODILS

By *William Wordsworth*

 WANDERED lonely as a cloud
That floats on high o'er vales
and hills,
When all at once I saw a crowd,
A host, of golden daffodils;
Beside the lake, beneath the trees,
Fluttering and dancing in the
breeze.

Continuous as the stars that shine
And twinkle on the milky way,
They stretched in never-ending line
Along the margin of a bay:
Ten thousand saw I at a glance,
Tossing their heads in sprightly dance.

The waves beside them danced, but they
Outdid the sparkling waves in glee;
A poet could not but be gay
In such a jocund company.
I gazed — and gazed — but little thought
What wealth the show to me had brought.

For oft, when on my couch I lie,
In vacant or in pensive mood,
They flash upon that inward eye
Which is the bliss of solitude;
And then my heart with pleasure fills,
And dances with the daffodils.

MY HEART LEAPS UP WHEN I BEHOLD

By William Wordsworth

Y heart leaps up when I behold
 A rainbow in the sky:
So was it when my life began;
So is it now I am a man;
So be it when I shall grow old,
 Or let me die!
The Child is father of the Man;
And I could wish my days to be
Bound each to each by natural piety.

"THE WORLD IS TOO MUCH WITH US"

By William Wordsworth

HE world is too much with us;
 late and soon,
Getting and spending, we lay
 waste our powers:
Little we see in Nature that is
 ours;
We have given our hearts away,
 a sordid boon!
This Sea that bares her bosom to the moon;
The winds that will be howling at all hours,
And are up-gathered now like sleeping flowers;
For this, for every thing, we are out of tune;

It moves us not. — Great God ! I'd rather be
A Pagan suckled in a creed outworn ;
So might I, standing on this pleasant lea,
Have glimpses that would make me less forlorn ;
Have sight of Proteus rising from the sea ;
Or hear old Triton blow his wreathèd horn.

TO A BUTTERFLY

By William Wordsworth

'VE watched you now a full half-
    hour,
Self-poised upon that yellow
    flower ;
And, little Butterfly ! indeed
I know not if you sleep or feed,
How motionless ! — not frozen
    seas
More motionless ! and then
What joy awaits you, when the breeze
Hath found you out among the trees,
And calls you forth again !

This plot of Orchard-ground is ours ;
My trees they are, my Sister's flowers ;
Here rest your wings when they are weary ;
Here lodge as in a sanctuary !
Come often to us, fear no wrong ;
Sit near us on the bough !
We'll talk of sunshine and of song,
And summer days, when we were young ;
Sweet childish days, that were as long
As twenty days are now.

AMONG THE HILLS

By John Greenleaf Whittier

FOR weeks the clouds had raked
    the hills
    And vexed the vales with
      raining,
    And all the woods were sad with
      mist,
    And all the brooks complain-
      ing.

At last, a sudden night-storm tore
    The mountain veils asunder,
And swept the valleys clean before
    The bosom of the thunder.

Through Sandwich notch the west-wind sang
    Good morrow to the cotter;
And once again Chocorua's horn
    Of shadow pierced the water.

Above his broad lake Ossipee,
    Once more the sunshine wearing,
Stooped, tracing on that silver shield
    His grim armorial bearing.

Clear drawn against the hard blue sky,
    The peaks had winter's keenness;
And close, on autumn's frost, the vales
    Had more than June's fresh greenness.

Again the sodden forest floors
    With golden lights were checkered,
Once more rejoicing leaves in wind
    And sunshine danced and flickered.

It was as if the summer's late
    Atoning for its sadness
Had borrowed every season's charm
    To end its days in gladness.

I call to mind those banded vales
    Of shadow and of shining,
Through which, my hostess at my side,
    I drove in day's declining.

We held our sideling way above
    The river's whitening shallows,
By homesteads old, with wide-flung barns
    Swept through and through by swallows;

By maple orchards, belts of pine
    And larches climbing darkly
The mountain slopes, and, over all,
    The great peaks rising starkly.

You should have seen that long hill-range
    With gaps of brightness riven, —
How through each pass and hollow streamed
    The purpling lights of heaven, —

Rivers of gold-mist flowing down
    From far celestial fountains, —
The great sun flaming through the rifts
    Beyond the wall of mountains!

We paused at last where home-bound cows
    Brought down the pasture's treasure,
And in the barn the rhythmic flails
    Beat out a harvest measure.

We heard the night-hawk's sullen plunge,
    The crow his tree-mates calling;
The shadows lengthening down the slopes
    About our feet were falling.

And through them smote the level sun
    In broken lines of splendor,
Touched the gray rocks and made the green
    Of the shorn grass more tender.

The maples bending o'er the gate,
    Their arch of leaves just tinted
With yellow warmth, the golden glow
    Of coming autumn hinted.

Keen white between the farm-house showed,
    And smiled on porch and trellis,
The fair democracy of flowers
    That equals cot and palace.

And weaving garlands for her dog,
    'Twixt chidings and caresses,
A human flower of childhood shook
    The sunshine from her tresses.

SNOW-BOUND

By John Greenleaf Whittier

HE sun that brief December day
Rose cheerless over hills of gray,
And, darkly circled, gave at noon
A sadder light than waning moon.
Slow tracing down the thickening sky
Its mute and ominous prophecy,
A portent seeming less than threat,
It sank from sight before it set.
A chill no coat, however stout,
Of homespun stuff could quite shut out.
A hard, dull bitterness of cold,
That checked, mid-vein, the circling race
Of life-blood in the sharpened face,
The coming of the snow-storm told.
The wind blew east ; we heard the roar
Of Ocean on his wintry shore,
And felt the strong pulse throbbing there
Beat with low rhythm our inland air.

Meanwhile we did our nightly chores, —
Brought in the wood from out of doors,
Littered the stalls, and from the mows
Raked down the herd's-grass for the cows ;
Heard the horse whinnying for his corn ;
And, sharply clashing horn on horn,

Impatient down the stanchion rows
The cattle shake their walnut bows;
While, peering from his early perch
Upon the scaffold's pole of birch,
The cock his crested helmet bent,
And down his querulous challenge sent.

Unwarmed by any sunset light
The gray day darkened into night,
A night made hoary with the swarm,
And whirl-dance of the blinding storm,
As zigzag, wavering to and fro,
Crossed and recrossed the wingèd snow:
And ere the early bedtime came
The white drift piled the window-frame,
And through the glass the clothes-line posts
Looked in like tall and sheeted ghosts.

So all night long the storm roared on:
The morning broke without a sun;
In tiny spherule traced with lines
Of Nature's geometric signs,
In starry flake and pellicle,
All day the hoary meteor fell;
And, when the second morning shone,
We looked upon a world unknown,
On nothing we could call our own.

Around the glistening wonder bent
The blue walls of the firmament,
No cloud above, no earth below, —
A universe of sky and snow!

The old familiar sights of ours
Took marvellous shapes; strange domes and towers
Rose up where sty or corn-crib stood,
Or garden-wall, or belt of wood;
A smooth white mound the brush-pile showed,
A fenceless drift what once was road;
The bridle-post an old man sat
With loose-flung coat and high cocked hat;
The well-curb had a Chinese roof;
And even the long sweep, high aloof
In its slant splendor, seemed to tell
Of Pisa's leaning miracle.

A prompt, decisive man, no breath
Our father wasted : " Boys, a path ! "
Well pleased (for when did farmer boy
Count such a summons less than joy ?)
Our buskins on our feet we drew;
With mittened hands, and caps drawn low,
To guard our necks and ears from snow,
We cut the solid whiteness through.
And, where the drift was deepest, made
A tunnel walled and overlaid
With dazzling crystal : we had read
Of rare Aladdin's wondrous cave,
And to our own his name we gave,
With many a wish the luck were ours
To test his lamp's supernal powers.
We reached the barn with merry din,
And roused the prisoned brutes within.
The old horse thrust his long head out,
And grave with wonder gazed about;

The cock his lusty greeting said,
And forth his speckled harem led ;
The oxen lashed their tails, and hooked,
And mild reproach of hunger looked;
The hornèd patriarch of the sheep,
Like Egypt's Amun roused from sleep,
Shook his sage head with gesture mute,
And emphasized with stamp of foot.

All day the gusty north-wind bore
The loosening drift its breath before ;
Low circling round its southern zone,
The sun through dazzling snow-mist shone.
No church-bell lent its Christian tone
To the savage air, no social smoke
Curled over woods of snow-hung oak.
A solitude made more intense
By dreary-voicèd elements,
The shrieking of the mindless wind,
The moaning tree-boughs swaying blind,
And on the glass the unmeaning beat
Of ghostly finger-tips of sleet.

Beyond the circle of our hearth
No welcome sound of toil or mirth
Unbound the spell, and testified
Of human life and thought outside.
We minded that the sharpest ear
The buried brooklet could not hear,
The music of whose liquid lip
Had been to us companionship,
And, in our lonely life, had grown
To have an almost human tone.

As night drew on, and, from the crest
Of wooded knolls that ridged the west,
The sun, a snow-blown traveller, sank
From sight beneath the smothering bank,
We piled, with care, our nightly stack
Of wood against the chimney-back, —
The oaken log, green, huge, and thick,
And on its top the stout back-stick;
The knotty fore-stick laid apart,
And filled between with curious art
The ragged brush; then, hovering near,
We watched the first red blaze appear,
Heard the sharp crackle, caught the gleam
On whitewashed wall and sagging beam
Until the old rude-furnished room
Burst, flower-like, into rosy bloom;
While radiant with a mimic flame
Outside the sparkling drift became,
And through the bare-boughed lilac-tree
Our own warm hearth seemed blazing free.
The crane and pendent trammels showed,
The Turks' heads on the andirons glowed;
While childish fancy prompt to tell
The meaning of the miracle,
Whispered the old rhyme: " *Under the tree,*
When fire outdoors burns merrily,
There the witches are making tea."

The moon above the eastern wood
Shone at its full; the hill-range stood
Transfigured in the silver flood,
Its blown snows flashing cold and keen,

Dead white, save where some sharp ravine
Took shadow, or the sombre green
Of hemlocks turned to pitchy black
Against the whiteness at their back.
For such a world and such a night
Most fitting that unwarming light,
Which only seemed where'er it fell
To make the coldness visible.

Shut in from all the world without,
We sat the clean-winged hearth about,
Content to let the north-wind roar
In baffled rage at pane and door,
While the red logs before us beat
The frost-line back with tropic heat;
And ever, when a louder blast
Shook beam and rafter as it passed,
The merrier up its roaring draught
The great throat of the chimney laughed;
The house-dog on his paws outspread
Laid to the fire his drowsy head,
The cat's dark silhouette on the wall
A couchant tiger's seemed to fall;
And, for the winter fireside meet,
Between the andirons' straddling feet,
The mug of cider simmered slow,
The apples sputtered in a row,
And, close at hand, the basket stood
With nuts from brown October's wood.

THE BAREFOOT BOY*

By John Greenleaf Whittier

LESSINGS on thee, little man,
Barefoot boy, with cheek of tan !
With thy turned-up pantaloons,
And thy merry whistled tunes ;
With thy red lip, redder still
Kissed by strawberries on the
hill ;
With the sunshine on thy face,
Through thy torn brim's jaunty grace ;
From my heart I give thee joy, —
I was once a barefoot boy !
Prince thou art, — the grown-up man
Only is republican.
Let the million-dollared ride !
Barefoot, trudging at his side,
Thou hast more than he can buy
In the reach of ear and eye, —
Outward sunshine, inward joy ;
Blessings on thee, barefoot boy !

Oh for boyhood's painless play,
Sleep that wakes in laughing day,
Health that mocks the doctor's rules,
Knowledge never learned of schools,
Of the wild bee's morning chase,
Of the wild-flower's time and place,

* The Poetical Works of John Greenleaf Whittier.   Ticknor &
Fields, 1869.

Flight of fowl and habitude
Of the tenants of the wood;
How the tortoise bears his shell,
How the woodchuck digs his cell,
And the ground-mole sinks his well;
How the robin feeds her young,
How the oriole's nest is hung;
Where the whitest lilies blow,
Where the freshest berries grow,
Where the groundnut trails its vine,
Where the wood-grape's clusters shine;
Of the black wasp's cunning way,
Mason of his walls of clay,
And the architectural plans
Of gray hornet artisans! —
For, eschewing books and tasks,
Nature answers all he asks;
Hand in hand with her he walks,
Face to face with her he talks,
Part and parcel of her joy, —
Blessings on the barefoot boy!

Oh for boyhood's time of June,
Crowding years in one brief moon,
When all things I heard or saw,
Me, their master, waited for.
I was rich in flowers and trees,
Humming-birds and honey-bees;
For my sport the squirrel played,
Plied the snouted mole his spade;
For my taste the blackberry cone
Purpled over hedge and stone;

Laughed the brook for my delight
Through the day and through the night,
Whispering at the garden wall,
Talked with me from fall to fall;
Mine the sand-rimmed pickerel pond,
Mine the walnut slopes beyond,
Mine, on bending orchard trees,
Apples of Hesperides!
Still as my horizon grew,
Larger grew my riches too;
All the world I saw or knew
Seemed a complex Chinese toy,
Fashioned for a barefoot boy!

Oh for festal dainties spread,
Like my bowl of milk and bread; —
Pewter spoon and bowl of wood,
On the door-stone, gray and rude!
O'er me, like a regal tent,
Cloudy-ribbed, the sunset bent,
Purple-curtained, fringed with gold,
Looped in many a wind-swung fold;
While for music came the play
Of the pied frogs' orchestra;
And, to light the noisy choir,
Lit the fly his lamp of fire.
I was monarch; pomp and joy
Waited on the barefoot boy!

Cheerily, then, my little man,
Live and laugh, as boyhood can!
Though the flinty slopes be hard,
Stubble-speared the new-mown sward,

Every morn shall lead thee through
Fresh baptisms of the dew;
Every evening from thy feet
Shall the cool wind kiss the heat;
All too soon these feet must hide
In the prison cells of pride,
Lose the freedom of the sod,
Like a colt's for work be shod,
Made to tread the mills of toil,
Up and down in ceaseless moil;
Happy if their track be found
Never on forbidden ground;
Happy if they sink not in
Quick and treacherous sands of sin.
Ah! that thou couldst know thy joy,
Ere it passes, barefoot boy!

THE BOBOLINK

By *Thomas Hill*

OBOLINK! that in the mead-
ow,
Or beneath the orchard's shadow,
Keepest up a constant rattle
Joyous as my children's prattle,
Welcome to the north again!
Welcome to mine ear thy strain,
Welcome to mine eye the sight
Of thy buff, thy black and white.

Brighter plumes may greet the sun
By the banks of Amazon;
Sweeter tones may weave the spell
Of enchanting Philomel;
But the tropic bird would fail,
And the English nightingale,
If we should compare their worth
With thine endless, gushing mirth.

When the ides of May are past,
June and summer nearing fast,
While from depths of blue above
Comes the mighty breath of love,
Calling out each bud and flower
With resistless, secret power, —
Waking hope and fond desire,
Kindling the erotic fire, —
Filling youths' and maidens' dreams
With mysterious, pleasing themes;
Then, amid the sunlight clear
Floating in the fragrant air,
Thou dost fill each heart with pleasure
By thy glad ecstatic measure.

A single note, so sweet and low,
Like a full heart's overflow,
Forms the prelude; but the strain
Gives us no such tone again;
For the wild and saucy song
Leaps and skips the notes among,
With such quick and sportive play,
Ne'er was madder, merrier lay.

Gayest songster of the spring!
Thy melodies before me bring
Visions of some dream-built land,
Where, by constant zephyrs fanned,
I might walk the livelong day,
Embosomed in perpetual May.
Nor care nor fear thy bosom knows;
For thee a tempest never blows;
But when our northern summer's o'er,
By Delaware's or Schuylkill's shore
The wild rice lifts its airy head,
And royal feasts for thee are spread.
And when the winter threatens there,
Thy tireless wings yet own no fear,
But bear thee to more southern coasts,
Far beyond the reach of frosts.
Bobolink! still may thy gladness
Take from me all taints of sadness;
Fill my soul with trust unshaken
In that Being who has taken
Care for every living thing,
In Summer, Winter, Fall, and Spring.

THE VESPER SPARROW

By Edith M. Thomas

IT comes from childhood land,
    Where summer days are long
And summer eves are bland, —
    A lulling good-night song.

Upon a pasture stone,
  Against the fading west,
A small bird sings alone,
  Then dives and finds its nest.

The evening star has heard,
  And flutters into sight;
O childhood's vesper-bird,
  My heart calls back, Good-Night.

THE GRASSHOPPER

By Edith M. Thomas

 HUTTLE of the sunburnt grass,
Fifer in the dun cuirass,
Fifing shrilly in the morn,
Shrilly still at eve unworn;
Now to rear, now in the van,
Gayest of the elfin clan:
Though I watch their rustling
        flight,
I can never guess aright
Where their lodging-places are;
'Mid some daisy's golden star,
Or beneath a roofing leaf,
Or in fringes of a sheaf,
Tenanted as soon as bound!
Loud thy reveille doth sound,
When the earth is laid asleep,
And her dreams are passing deep,

Or mid-August afternoons;
And through all the harvest moons,
Nights brimmed up with honeyed peace,
Thy gainsaying doth not cease.
When the frost comes, thou art dead;
We along the stubble tread,
On blue, frozen morns, and note
No least murmur is afloat:
Wondrous still our fields are then,
Fifer of the elfin men !

A WORD WITH A SKYLARK

By Sarah Piatt

(A Caprice of Homesickness.)

IF this be all, for which I've lis-
    tened long,
    Oh, spirit of the dew !
You did not sing to Shelley such
    a song
    As Shelley sung to you.

Yet, with this ruined Old World for a nest,
    Worm-eaten through and through, —
This waste of grave-dust stamped with crown and
    crest, —
    What better could you do ?

Ah me ! but when the world and I were young,
    There was an apple-tree,
There was a voice came in the dawn and sung
    The buds awake — ah me !

Oh, Lark of Europe, downward fluttering near,
    Like some spent leaf at best,
You'd never sing again if you could hear
    My Blue-Bird of the West!

IN THE HAUNTS OF BASS AND BREAM

By Maurice Thompson

I

D REAMS come true, and every-
        thing
    Is fresh and lusty in the spring.

In groves, that smell like am-
        bergris,
Wind-songs, bird-songs, never cease.

Go with me down by the stream,
Haunt of bass and purple bream;

Feel the pleasure, keen and sweet,
When the cool waves lap your feet;

Catch the breath of moss and mould,
Hear the grosbeak's whistle bold;

See the heron all alone
Mid-stream on a slippery stone,

Or, on some decaying log,
Spearing snail or water-frog;

See the shoals of sun-perch shine
Among the pebbles smooth and fine,

Whilst the sprawling turtles swim
In the eddies cool and dim !

II

The busy nuthatch climbs his tree,
Around the great bole spirally,

Peeping into wrinkles gray,
Under ruffled lichens gay,

Lazily piping one sharp note
From his silver mailèd throat ;

And down the wind the catbird's song
A slender medley trails along.

Here a grackle chirping low,
There a crested vireo ;

Deep in tangled underbrush
Flits the shadowy hermit-thrush ;

Cooes the dove, the robin trills,
The crows caw from the airy hills ;

Purple finch and pewee gray,
Blue-bird, swallow, oriole gay, —

Every tongue of Nature sings ;
The air is palpitant with wings !

Halcyon prophecies come to pass
In the haunts of bream and bass.

III

Bubble, bubble, flows the stream,
Like an old tune through a dream.

Now I cast my silken line;
See the gay lure spin and shine,

While with delicate touch I feel
The gentle pulses of the reel.

Halcyon laughs and cuckoo cries;
Through its leaves the plane-tree sighs.

Bubble, bubble, flows the stream,
Here a glow and there a gleam;

Coolness all about me creeping,
Fragrance all my senses steeping, —

Spicewood, sweet-gum, sassafras,
Calamus and water-grass,

Giving up their pungent smells,
Drawn from Nature's secret wells;

On the cool breath of the morn,
Perfume of the cock-spur thorn,

Green spathes of the dragon-root,
Indian turnip's tender shoot,

Dogwood, red-bud, elder, ash,
Snowy gleam and purple flash,

Hillside thickets, densely green,
That the partridge revels in!

IV

I see the morning-glory's curl,
The curious star-flower's pointed whorl;

Hear the woodpecker, rap-a-tap!
See him with his cardinal's cap!

And the querulous, leering jay,
How he clamors for a fray!

Patiently I draw and cast,
Keenly expectant till, at last,

Comes a flash, down in the stream,
Never made by perch or bream;

Then a mighty weight I feel,
Sings the line and whirs the reel!

V

Out of a giant tulip-tree
A great gay blossom falls on me;

Old gold and fire its petals are,
It flashes like a falling star.

A big blue heron flying by
Looks at me with a greedy eye.

I see a stripèd squirrel shoot
Into a hollow maple-root;

A bumble-bee with mail all rust,
His thighs puffed out with anther-dust,

Clasps a shrinking bloom about,
And draws her amber sweetness out.

VI

Bubble, bubble, flows the stream,
Like a song heard in a dream.

A white-faced hornet hurtles by,
Lags a turquoise butterfly, —

One intent on prey and treasure,
One afloat on tides of pleasure!

Sunshine arrows, swift and keen,
Pierce the burr-oak's helmet green.

VII

I follow where my victim leaps
Through tangles of rank water-weeds,

O'er stone and root and knotty log,
O'er faithless bits of reedy bog.

I wonder will he ever stop?
The reel hums like a humming top!

Through graceful curves he sweeps the line,
He sulks, he starts, his colors shine,

Whilst I, all flushed and breathless, tear
Through lady-fern and maiden's-hair,

And in my straining fingers feel
The throbbing of the rod and reel !

A thin sandpiper, wild with fright,
Goes into ecstasies of flight ;

A gaunt green bittern quits the rushes,
The yellow-throat its warbling hushes ;

Bubble, bubble, flows the stream,
Like an old tune through a dream !

VIII

At last he tires, I reel him in ;
I see the glint of scale and fin.

The crinkled halos round him break,
He leaves gay bubbles in his wake.

I raise the rod, I shorten line,
And safely land him, — he is mine !

IX

The belted halcyon laughs, the wren
Comes twittering from its brushy den ;

The turtle sprawls upon its log,
I hear the booming of a frog.

Liquidamber's keen perfume,
Sweet-punk, calamus, tulip bloom ;

Dancing wasp and dragon-fly,
Wood-thrush whistling tenderly ;

Damp cool breath of moss and mould,
Noontide's influence manifold ;

Glimpses of a cloudless sky, —
Soothe me as I resting lie.

Bubble, bubble, flows the stream,
Like low music through a dream.

A TOUCH OF NATURE

By Thomas Bailey Aldrich

 HEN first the crocus thrusts its
point of gold
Up through the still snow-
drifted garden mould,
And folded green things in dim
woods unclose
Their crinkled spears, a sudden
tremor goes
Into my veins and makes me kith and kin
To every wild-born thing that thrills and blows.
Sitting beside this crumbling sea-coal fire,
Here in the city's ceaseless roar and din,
Far from the brambly paths I used to know,
Far from the rustling brooks that slip and shine
Where the Neponset alders take their glow,
I share the tremulous sense of bud and briar
And inarticulate ardors of the vine.

SEA LONGINGS

By Thomas Bailey Aldrich

THE first world-sound that fell
    upon my ear
Was that of the great winds
    along the coast
Crushing the deep-sea beryl on
    the rocks —
The distant breakers' sullen
    cannonade.
Against the spires and gables of the town
The white fog drifted, catching here and there
At over-leaning cornice or peaked roof,
And hung — weird gonfalons. The garden walks
Were choked with leaves, and on their ragged
    biers
Lay dead the sweets of summer — damask rose,
Clove-pink, old-fashioned, loved New England
    flowers.

Only keen salt sea-odors filled the air.
Sea-sounds, sea-odors — these were all my world.
Hence is it that life languishes with me
Inland; the valleys stifle me with gloom
And pent-up prospects; in their narrow bound
Imagination flutters futile wings.
Vainly I seek the sloping pearl-white sand
And the mirage's phantom citadels
Miraculous, a moment seen, then gone.
Among the mountains I am ill at ease,

Missing the stretched horizon's level line
And the illimitable restless blue.
The crag-torn sky is not the sky I love,
But one unbroken sapphire spanning all;
And nobler than the branches of a pine
Aslant upon a precipice's edge
Are the strained spars of some great battle-ship
Plowing across the sunset.   No bird's lilt
So takes me as the whistling of the gale
Among the shrouds.   My cradle-song was this,
Strange inarticulate sorrows of the sea,
Blithe rhythms upgathered from the Sirens' caves.
Perchance of earthly voices the last voice
That shall an instant my freed spirit stay
On this world's verge, will be some message blown
Over the dim salt lands that fringe the coast
At dusk or when the trancëd midnight droops
With weight of stars, or haply just as dawn,
Illumining the sullen purple wave,
Turns the gray pools and willow-stems to gold.

THE BLUEBIRD

By Thomas Bailey Aldrich

(From " Spring in New England.")

HARK 'tis the bluebird's venturous strain
High on the old fringed elm at the gate —
Sweet-voiced, valiant on the swaying bough,
  Alert, elate,
Dodging the fitful spits of snow,
  New England's poet-laureate
Telling us Spring has come again !

SONG OF THE RIVER

By Charles Kingsley

CLEAR and cool, clear and cool,
  By laughing shallow, and dream-
    ing pool;
  Cool and clear, cool and clear,
  By shining shingle, and foaming
    wear;
  Under the crag where the ouzel
    sings,
And the ivied wall where the church-bell rings,
Undefiled, for the undefiled;
Play by me, bathe in me, mother and child.

Dank and foul, dank and foul,
By the smoky town in its murky cowl;
Foul and dank, foul and dank,
By wharf and sewer and slimy bank;
Darker and darker the further I go,
Baser and baser the richer I grow;
Who dare sport with the sin-defiled?
Shrink from me, turn from me, mother and child.

Strong and free, strong and free,
The floodgates are open, away to the sea,
Free and strong, free and strong,
Cleansing my streams as I hurry along
To the golden sands, and the leaping bar,
And the taintless tide that awaits me afar,

As I lose myself in the infinite main,
Like a soul that has sinned and is pardoned again.
Undefiled, for the undefiled;
Play by me, bathe in me, mother and child.

THE ROSE IN OCTOBER

By Mary Townley

 LATE and sweet, too sweet, too late !
What nightingale will sing to thee ?
The empty nest, the shivering tree,
The dead leaves by the garden gate,
And cawing crows for thee will wait,
O sweet and late !

Where wert thou when the soft June nights
Were faint with perfume, glad with song ?
Where wert thou when the days were long
And steeped in summer's young delights ?
What hopest thou now but checks and slights,
Brief days, lone nights ?

Stay ! there's a gleam of winter wheat
Far on the hill; down in the woods
A very heaven of stillness broods ;
And through the mellow sun's noon heat,
Lo, tender pulses round thee beat,
O late and sweet !

NOVEMBER

By C. L. Cleaveland

HEN thistle-blows do lightly float
About the pasture-height,
And shrills the hawk a parting note,
And creeps the frost at night,
Then hilly ho! though singing so,
And whistle as I may,
There comes again the old heart pain
Through all the livelong day.

In high wind creaks the leafless tree
And nods the fading fern ;
The knolls are dun as snow-clouds be,
And cold the sun does burn.
Then ho, hollo! though calling so,
I cannot keep it down ;
The tears arise unto my eyes,
And thoughts are chill and brown.

Far in the cedars' dusky stoles,
Where the sere ground-vine weaves,
The partridge drums funereal rolls
Above the fallen leaves.
And hip, hip, ho! though cheering so,
It stills no whit the pain ;
For drip, drip, drip, from bare branch-tip,
I hear the year's last rain.

So drive the cold cows from the hill,
And call the wet sheep in;
And let their stamping clatter fill
The barn with warming din.
And ho, folk, ho! though it is so
That we no more may roam,
We still will find a cheerful mind
Around the fire at home!

THE HUMMING-BIRD

By Ednah Proctor Clarke

ANCER of air,
    Flashing thy flight across the
        noontide hour,
    To pierce and pass ere it is full
        aware
    Each wondering flower!

Jewelled coryphée,
With quivering wings like shielding gauze out-
    spread,
And measure like a gleaming shuttle's play
        With unseen thread!

The phlox, milk-white,
Sways to thy whirling; stirs each warm rose breast;
But not for these thy palpitant delight,
        Thy rhythmic quest;

Swift weaves thy maze
Where flaunts the trumpet-vine its scarlet pride,
Where softer fire, behind its chaliced blaze,
        Doth fluttering hide.

The grave thrush sings
His love-call, and the nightingale's romance
Throbs through the twilight; thou hast but thy
    wings,
        Thy sun-thrilled dance.

        Yet doth love's glow
Burn in the ruby of thy restless throat,
Guiding thy voiceless ecstasy to know
        The richest note

        Of brooding thrush!
Now for thy joy the emptied air doth long;
Thine is the nested silence, and the hush
        That needs no song.

FOOTPRINTS IN THE SNOW

By Frank Dempster Sherman

WORN is the winter rug of white,
    And in the snow-bare spots
      once more
Glimpses of faint green grass in
    sight, —
    Spring's footprints on the
    floor.

Upon the sombre forest gates
  A crimson flush the mornings catch,
The token of the Spring, who waits
  With finger on the latch.

Blow, bugles of the south, and win
    The warders from their dreams too long,
And bid them let the new guest in
    With her glad hosts of song.

She shall make bright the dismal ways
    With broideries of bud and bloom,
With music fill the nights and days
    And end the garden's gloom.

Her face is lovely with the sun ;
    Her voice — ah, listen to it now !
The silence of the year is done :
    The bird is on the bough !

Spring here, — by what magician's touch ?
    'Twas winter scarce an hour ago.
And yet I should have guessed as much, —
    Those footprints in the snow !

TO THE CAT-BIRD

Anonymous

YOU, who would with wanton art
    Counterfeit another's part,
    And with noisy utterance claim
Right to an ignoble name, —
Inharmonious ! — why must you,
To a better self untrue,
Gifted with the charm of song,
Do the generous gift such wrong ?

Delicate and downy throat,
Shaped for pure, melodious note, —
Silvery wings of softest gray, —
Bright eyes glancing every way, —
Graceful outline, — motion free :
Types of perfect harmony !

Ah ! you much mistake your duty,
Mating discord thus with beauty, —
'Mid these heavenly sunset gleams,
Vexing the smooth air with screams, —
Burdening the dainty breeze
With insane discordancies.

I have heard you tell a tale
Tender as the nightingale,
Sweeter than the early thrush
Pipes at day-dawn from the bush.
Wake once more the liquid strain
That you poured, like music-rain,
When, last night, in the sweet weather,
You and I were out together.

Unto whom two notes are given,
One of earth, and one of heaven,
Were it not a shameful tale
That the earth-note should prevail ?

For the sake of those who love us,
For the sake of God above us,
Each and all should do their best
To make music for the rest.

So will I no more reprove,
Though the chiding be in love :
Uttering harsh rebuke to you,
That were inharmonious, too.

THE WHITE-THROATED SPARROW

By A. West

HARK ! 't is our Northern Night-
ingale that sings
In far-off, leafy cloisters, dark
and cool,
Flinging his flute-notes bounding
from the skies !

Thou wild musician of the
mountain-streams,
Most tuneful minstrel of the forest-choirs,
Bird of all grace and harmony of soul,
Unseen, we hail thee for thy blissful voice !

Up in yon tremulous mist where morning wakes
Illimitable shadows from their dark abodes,
Or in this woodland glade tumultuous grown
With all the murmurous language of the trees,
No blither presence fills the vocal space.
The wandering rivulets dancing through the grass,
The gambols, low or loud, of insect-life,
The cheerful call of cattle in the vales,
Sweet natural sounds of the contented hours, —
All seem less jubilant when thy song begins.

Deep in the shade we lie and listen long;
For human converse well may pause, and man
Learn from such notes fresh hints of praise,
That upward swelling from thy grateful tribe
Circles the hills with melodies of joy.

A CAGED BIRD

By Sarah Orne Jewett

HIGH at the window in her cage
    The old canary flits and sings,
Nor sees across the curtain pass
    The shadow of a swallow's
        wings.

A poor deceit and copy, this,
  Of larger lives that mark their span,
Unreckoning of wider worlds
  Or gifts that Heaven keeps for man.

She gathers piteous bits and shreds,
  This solitary, mateless thing,
To patient build again the nest
  So rudely scattered spring by spring;

And sings her brief, unlistened songs,
  Her dreams of bird-life wild and free,
Yet never beats her prison bars
  At sound of song from bush or tree.

But in my busiest hours I pause,
    Held by a sense of urgent speech,
Bewildered by that spark-like soul,
    Able my very soul to reach.

She will be heard; she chirps me loud,
    When I forget those gravest cares,
Her small provision to supply,
    Clear water or her seedsman's wares.

She begs me now for that chief joy
    The round great world is made to grow, —
Her wisp of greenness.   Hear her chide,
    Because my answering thought is slow!

What can my life seem like to her?
    A dull, unpunctual service mine;
Stupid before her eager call,
    Her flitting steps, her insight fine.

To open wide thy prison door,
    Poor friend, would give thee to thy foes;
And yet a plaintive note I hear,
    As if to tell how slowly goes

The time of thy long prisoning.
    Bird! does some promise keep thee sane?
Will there be better days for thee?
    Will thy soul too know life again?

Ah, none of us have more than this:
    If one true friend green leaves can reach
From out some fairer, wider place,
    And understand our wistful speech.

BLOOD-ROOT

By E. S. F.

WHEN 'mid the budding elms the
bluebird flits,
As if a bit of sky had taken
wings;
When cheerily the first brave
robin sings,
While timid April smiles and
weeps by fits,
Then dainty Blood-Root dons her pale-green wrap,
And ventures forth in some warm, sheltered nook,
To sit and listen to the gurgling brook,
And rouse herself from her long winter nap.
Give her a little while to muse and dream,
And she will throw her leafy cloak aside,
And stand in shining raiment, like a bride
Waiting her lord; whiter than snow will seem
Her spotless robe, the moss-grown rocks beside,
And bright as morn her golden crown will gleam.

THE PASSING OF MARCH

By Robert Burns Wilson

THE braggart March stood in the season's
door
With his broad shoulders blocking up
the way,
Shaking the snow-flakes from the cloak he wore,
And from the fringes of his kirtle gray.

Near by him April stood with tearful face,
　　With violets in her hands, and in her hair
Pale, wild anemones; the fragrant lace
　　Half-parted from her breast, which seemed like fair,
Dawn-tinted mountain snow, smooth-drifted there.

She on the blusterer's arm laid one white hand,
　　But he would none of her soft blandishment,
Yet did she plead with tears none might understand,
　　For even the fiercest hearts at last relent.
And he, at last, in ruffian tenderness,
　　With one swift, crushing kiss her lips did greet,
Ah, poor starved heart! — for that one rude caress,
　　She cast her violets underneath his feet.

WHEN IN THE NIGHT WE WAKE AND HEAR THE RAIN

By Robert Burns Wilson

HEN in the night we wake and hear the rain
　　Like myriad merry footfalls on the grass,
And, on the roof, the friendly, threatening crash
　　Of sweeping, cloud-sped messengers, that pass
Far through the clamoring night; or loudly dash
Against the rattling windows; storming, still
In swift recurrence, each dim-streaming pane,

Insistent that the dreamer wake, within,
And dancing in the darkness on the sill:
How is it, then, with us — amidst the din,
  Recalled from Sleep's dim, vision-swept do-
    main —
  When in the night we wake and hear the rain?

When in the night we wake and hear the rain,
Like mellow music, comforting the earth;
A muffled, half-elusive serenade,
Too softly sung for grief, too grave for mirth;
Such as night-wandering fairy minstrels made
In fabled, happier days; while far in space
The serious thunder rolls a deep refrain,
Jarring the forest, wherein Silence makes
Amidst the stillness her lone dwelling-place;
Then in the soul's sad consciousness awakes
  Some nameless chord, touched by that haunt-
    ing strain,
  When in the night we wake and hear the rain.

When in the night we wake and hear the rain,
And from blown casements see the lightning sweep
The ocean's breadth with instantaneous fire,
Dimpling the lingering curve of waves that creep
In steady tumult — waves that never tire
For vexing, night and day, the glistening rocks,
Firm-fixed in their immovable disdain
Against the sea's alternate rage and play:
Comes there not something on the wind which
  mocks
The feeble thoughts, the foolish aims that sway

Our souls with hopes of unenduring gain —
When in the night we wake and hear the
    rain?

When in the night we wake and hear the rain
Which on the white bloom of the orchard falls,
And on the young, green wheat-blades, nodding
    now,
And on the half-turned field, where thought re-
    calls
How in the furrow stands the rusting plow,
Then fancy pictures what the day will see —
The ducklings paddling in the puddled lane,
Sheep grazing slowly up the emerald slope,
Clear bird-notes ringing, and the droning bee
Among the lilacs' bloom — enchanting hope —
    How fair the fading dreams we entertain,
    When in the night we wake and hear the rain !

When in the night we wake and hear the rain
Which falls on Summer's ashes, when the leaves
Are few and fading, and the fields forlorn
No more remember their long-gathered sheaves,
Nor aught of all the gladness they have worn ;
When melancholy veils the misty hills
Where sombre Autumn's latest glories wane ;
Then goes the soul forth where the sad year lays
On Summer's grave her withered gifts, and fills
Her urn with broken memories of sweet days —
    Dear days which, being vanished, yet remain,
    When in the night we wake and hear the
    rain.

When in the night we wake not with the rain —
When Silence, like a watchful shade, will keep
Too well her vigil by the lonely bed
In which at last we rest in quiet sleep ;
While from the sod the melted snows be shed,
And Spring's green grass, with Summer's ripening
    sun,
Grows brown and matted like a lion's mane,
How will it be with us ? No more to care
Along the journeying wind's wild path to run
When Nature's voice shall call, no more to share
    Love's madness — no regret — no longings
      vain —
    When in the night we wake not with the rain.

DOVER BEACH

By Matthew Arnold

THE sea is calm to-night.
    The tide is full, the moon lies
      fair
    Upon the straits ; — on the
      French coast the light
    Gleams and is gone ; the cliffs of
      England stand,
Glimmering and vast, out in the tranquil bay.
Come to the window, sweet is the night-air !
Only, from the long line of spray
Where the sea meets the moon-blanch'd land,
Listen ! you hear the grating roar

Of pebbles which the waves draw back, and fling,
At their return, up the high strand,
Begin, and cease, and then again begin,
With tremulous cadence slow, and bring
The eternal note of sadness in.

Sophocles long ago
Heard it on the Ægæan, and it brought
Into his mind the turbid ebb and flow
Of human misery ; we
Find also in the sound a thought,
Hearing it by this distant northern sea.

The sea of faith
Was once, too, at the full, and round earth's
     shore
Lay like the folds of a bright girdle furl'd.
But now I only hear
Its melancholy, long, withdrawing roar,
Retreating, to the breath
Of the night-wind, down the vast edges drear
And naked shingles of the world.

Ah, love, let us be true
To one another ! for the world, which seems
To lie before us like a land of dreams,
So various, so beautiful, so new,
Hath really neither joy, nor love, nor light,
Nor certitude, nor peace, nor help for pain ;
And we are here as on a darkling plain
Swept with confused alarms of struggle and flight,
Where ignorant armies clash by night.

POOR MATTHIAS

By *Matthew Arnold*

POOR Matthias! — Found him
  lying
Fall'n beneath his perch and
  dying?
Found him stiff, you say, though
  warm —
All convulsed his little form?
Poor canary! many a year
Well he knew his mistress dear;
Now in vain you call his name,
Vainly raise his rigid frame,
Vainly warm him in your breast,
Vainly kiss his golden crest,
Smooth his ruffled plumage fine,
Touch his trembling beak with wine.
One more gasp — it is the end!
Dead and mute our tiny friend!
— Songster thou of many a year,
Now thy mistress brings thee here,
Says, it fits that I rehearse,
Tribute due to thee, a verse,
Mead for daily song of yore
Silent now for evermore.

Poor Matthias! Wouldst thou have
More than pity? claim'st a stave?
— Friends more near us than a bird
We dismiss'd without a word.

Rover, with the good brown head,
Great Atossa, they are dead;
Dead, and neither prose nor rhyme
Tells the praises of their prime.
Thou didst know them old and grey,
Know them in their sad decay.
Thou hast seen Atossa sage
Sit for hours beside thy cage;
Thou wouldst chirp, thou foolish bird,
Flutter, chirp — she never stirr'd!
What were now these toys to her?
Down she sank amid her fur;
Eyed thee with a soul resign'd —
And thou deemedst cats were kind!
— Cruel, but composed and bland,
Dumb, inscrutable and grand,
So Tiberius might have sat,
Had Tiberius been a cat.

Rover died — Atossa too.
Less than they to us are you!
Nearer human were their powers,
Closer knit their life with ours.
Hands had stroked them, which are cold,
Now for years, in churchyard mould;
Comrades of our past were they,
Of that unreturning day.
Changed and aging, they and we
Dwelt, it seem'd, in sympathy.
Alway from their presence broke
Somewhat which remembrance woke

Of the loved, the lost, the young —
Yet they died, and died unsung.

Geist came next, our little friend;
Geist had verse to mourn his end.
Yes, but that enforcement strong
Which compell'd for Geist a song —
All that gay courageous cheer,
All that human pathos dear;
Soul-fed eyes with suffering worn,
Pain heroically borne,
Faithful love in depth divine —
Poor Matthias, were they thine?

Max and Kaiser we to-day
Greet upon the lawn at play;
Max a dachshund without blot —
Kaiser should be, but is not.
Max, with shining yellow coat,
Prinking ears and dewlap throat —
Kaiser, with his collie face,
Penitent for want of race.
— Which may be the first to die,
Vain to augur, they or I!
But, as age comes on, I know,
Poet's fire gets faint and low;
If so be that travel they
First the inevitable way,
Much I doubt if they shall have
Dirge from me to crown their grave.

Yet, poor bird, thy tiny corse
Moves me, somehow, to remorse;

Something haunts my conscience, brings
Sad, compunctious visitings.
Other favourites, dwelling here,
Open lived to us, and near;
Well we knew when they were glad,
Plain we saw if they were sad,
Joy'd with them when they were gay,
Soothed them in their last decay;
Sympathy could feel and show
Both in weal of theirs and woe.

Birds, companions more unknown,
Live beside us, but alone;
Finding not, do all they can,
Passage from their souls to man.
Kindness we bestow, and praise,
Laud their plumage, greet their lays;
Still, beneath their feather'd breast,
Stirs a history unexpress'd.
Wishes there, and feelings strong,
Incommunicably throng;
What they want, we cannot guess,
Fail to track their deep distress —
Dull look on when death is nigh,
Note no change, and let them die.
Poor Matthias! couldst thou speak,
What a tale of thy last week!
Every morning did we pay
Stupid salutations gay,
Suited well to health, but how
Mocking, how incongruous now!

Cake we offer'd, sugar, seed,
Never doubtful of thy need;
Praised, perhaps, thy courteous eye,
Praised thy golden livery.
Gravely thou the while, poor dear!
Sat'st upon thy perch to hear,
Fixing with a mute regard
Us, thy human keepers hard,
Troubling, with our chatter vain,
Ebb of life, and mortal pain —
Us, unable to divine
Our companion's dying sign,
Or o'erpass the severing sea
Set betwixt ourselves and thee,
Till the sand thy feathers smirch
Fallen dying off thy perch!

Was it, as the Grecian sings,
Birds were born the first of things,
Before the sun, before the wind,
Before the gods, before mankind,
Airy, ante-mundane throng —
Witness their unworldly song!
Proof they give, too, primal powers,
Of a prescience more than ours —
Teach us, while they come and go,
When to sail, and when to sow.
Cuckoo calling from the hill,
Swallow skimming by the mill,
Swallows trooping in the sedge,
Starlings swirling from the hedge,

Mark the seasons, map our year,
As they show and disappear.
But, with all this travail sage
Brought from that anterior age,
Goes an unreversed decree
Whereby strange are they and we,
Making want of theirs, and plan,
Indiscernible by man.

No, away with tales like these
Stol'n from Aristophanes!
Does it, if we miss your mind,
Prove us so remote in kind?
Birds! we but repeat on you
What amongst ourselves we do.
Somewhat more or somewhat less,
'Tis the same unskilfulness.
What you feel, escapes our ken —
Know we more our fellow men?
Human suffering at our side,
Ah, like yours is undescried!
Human longings, human fears,
Miss our eyes and miss our ears.
Little helping, wounding much,
Dull of heart, and hard of touch,
Brother man's despairing sign
Who may trust us to divine?
Who assure us, sundering powers
Stand not 'twixt his soul and ours?

Poor Matthias! See, thy end
What a lesson doth it lend!

For that lesson thou shalt have,
Dead canary bird, a stave!
Telling how, one stormy day,
Stress of gale and showers of spray
Drove my daughter small and me
Inland from the rocks and sea.
Driv'n inshore, we follow down
Ancient streets of Hastings town —
Slowly thread them — when behold,
French canary-merchant old
Shepherding his flock of gold
In a low dim-lighted pen
Scann'd of tramps and fishermen!
There a bird, high-colored, fat,
Proud of port, though something squat —
Pursy, play'd-out Philistine —
Dazzled Nelly's youthful eyne.
But, far in, obscure, there stirr'd
On his perch a sprightlier bird,
Courteous-eyed, erect and slim;
And I whisper'd: "Fix on *him!*"
Home we brought him, young and fair,
Songs to thrill in Surrey air.
Here Matthias sang his fill,
Saw the cedars of Pains Hill;
Here he pour'd his little soul,
Heard the murmur of the Mole.
Eight in number now the years
He hath pleased our eyes and ears;
Other favorites he hath known
Go, and now himself is gone.

— Fare thee well, companion dear!
Fare for ever well, nor fear,
Tiny though thou art, to stray
Down the uncompanion'd way!
We without thee, little friend,
Many years have not to spend;
What are left, will hardly be
Better than we spent with thee.

THE DEPARTURE OF THE CUCKOO

(From "Thyrsis")

By Matthew Arnold

S̲O, some tempestuous morn in
    early June,
    When the year's primal burst
    of bloom is o'er,
Before the roses and the longest
    day —
    When garden-walks and all
    the grassy floor
With blossoms red and white of fallen May
And chestnut-flowers are strewn —
So have I heard the cuckoo's parting cry,
    From the wet field, through the vext garden-
    trees,
    Come with the volleying rain and tossing breeze:
The bloom is gone, and with the bloom go I!

PHILOMELA

By Matthew Arnold

ARK ! ah, the nightingale —
The tawny-throated !
Hark, from that moonlit cedar
what a burst !
What triumph ! hark ! — what
pain !

O wanderer from a Grecian shore,
Still, after many years, in distant lands,
Still nourishing in thy bewildered brain
That wild, unquench'd, deep-sunken, old-world
pain —
Say, will it never heal ?
And can this fragrant lawn,
With its cool trees, and night,
And the sweet, tranquil Thames,
And moonshine, and the dew,
To thy rack'd heart and brain
 Afford no balm ?

Dost thou to-night behold,
Here, through the moonlight on this English grass,
The unfriendly palace in the Thracian wild ?
Dost thou again peruse
With hot cheeks and seared eyes
The too clear web, and thy dumb sister's shame !
Dost thou once more essay

Thy flight, and feel come over thee,
Poor fugitive, the feathery change
Once more, and once more make resound,
With love and hate, triumph and agony,
Lone Daulis, and the high Cephissian vale?
Listen, Eugenia —
How thick the bursts come crowding through the
    leaves !
Again — thou hearest?
Eternal passion !
Eternal pain !

TRAILING ARBUTUS

By Henry Abbey

IN spring, when branches of woodbine
    Hung leafless over the rocks,
And the fleecy snow in the hollows
    Lay in unshepherded flocks,

By the road where the dead leaves rustled,
    Or damply matted the ground,
While over me lifted the robin
    His honeyed passion of sound,

I saw the trailing arbutus
    Blooming in modesty sweet,
And gathered store of its richness
    Offered and spread at my feet.

It grew under leaves, as if seeking
   No hint of itself to disclose,
And out of its pink-white petals
   A delicate perfume rose,

As faint as the fond remembrance
   Of joy that was only dreamed;
And like a divine suggestion
   The scent of the flower seemed.

I had sought for love on the highway,
   For love unselfish and pure,
And had found it in good deeds blooming,
   Though often in haunts obscure.

Often in leaves by the wayside,
   But touched with a heavenly glow,
And with self-sacrifice fragrant,
   The flowers of great love grow.

O lovely and lowly arbutus!
   As year unto year succeeds,
Be thou the laurel and emblem
   Of noble, unselfish deeds.

WINTER DAYS

By Henry Abbey

NOW comes the graybeard of the north:
   The forests bare their rugged breasts
   To every wind that wanders forth,
And, in their arms, the lonely nests
That housed the birdlings months ago
Are egged with flakes of drifted snow.

No more the robin pipes his lay
   To greet the flushed advance of morn;
He sings in valleys far away;
His heart is with the south to-day;
   He cannot shrill among the corn:
For all the hay and corn are down
   And garnered; and the withered leaf,
Against the branches bare and brown,
   Rattles; and all the days are brief.

An icy hand is on the land;
   The cloudy sky is sad and gray;
But through the misty sorrow streams
   A heavenly and golden ray.
And on the brook that cuts the plain
   A diamond wonder is aglow,
   Fairer than that which, long ago,
De Rohan staked a name to gain.

ROBIN'S COME!

By William W. Caldwell

FROM the elm-tree's topmost bough,
   Hark! the Robin's early song!
   Telling one and all that now
Merry spring-time hastes along;
Welcome tidings dost thou bring,
Little harbinger of spring,
       Robin's come!

Of the winter we are weary,
　　Weary of the frost and snow,
Longing for the sunshine cheery,
　　And the brooklet's gurgling flow;
Gladly then we hear thee sing
The reveillé of spring,
　　　　　　　　Robin's come!

Ring it out o'er hill and plain,
　　Through the garden's lonely bowers,
Till the green leaves dance again,
　　Till the air is sweet with flowers!
Wake the cowslips by the rill,
Wake the yellow daffodil!
　　　　　　　　Robin's come!

Then as thou wert wont of yore,
　　Build thy nest and rear thy young,
Close beside our cottage door,
　　In the woodbine leaves among;
Hurt or harm thou need'st not fear,
Nothing rude shall venture near.
　　　　　　　　Robin's come!

Swinging still o'er yonder lane
　　Robin answers merrily;
Ravished by the sweet refrain,
　　Alice claps her hands in glee,
Calling from the open door,
With her soft voice, o'er and o'er,
　　　　　　　　Robin's come!

TO A SEA-BIRD

By Francis Bret Harte

AUNTERING hither on listless
    wings,
  Careless vagabond of the sea,
Little thou heedest the surf that
    sings,
The bar that thunders, the shale
    that rings, —
  Give me to keep thy company.

Little thou hast, old friend, that's new;
  Storms and wrecks are old things to thee;
Sick am I of these changes too;
Little to care for, little to rue, —
  I on the shore, and thou on the sea.

All of thy wanderings, far and near,
  Bring thee at last to shore and me;
All of my journeyings end them here,
This our tether must be our cheer, —
  I on the shore, and thou on the sea.

Lazily rocking on ocean's breast,
  Something in common, old friend, have we;
Thou on the shingle seekest thy nest,
I to the waters look for rest, —
  I on the shore, and thou on the sea.

GRIZZLY

By Francis Bret Harte

COWARD, — of heroic size,
In whose lazy muscles lies
Strength we fear and yet despise;
Savage, — whose relentless tusks
Are content with acorn husks;
Robber, — whose exploits ne'er
    soared
O'er the bee's or squirrel's hoard;
Whiskered chin, and feeble nose,
Claws of steel on baby toes, —
Here, in solitude and shade,
Shambling, shuffling plantigrade,
Be thy courses undismayed!

Here, where Nature makes thy bed,
Let thy rude, half-human tread
   Point to hidden Indian springs,
Lost in ferns and fragrant grasses,
   Hovered o'er by timid wings,
Where the wood-duck lightly passes,
Where the wild bee holds her sweets, —
Epicurean retreats,
Fit for thee, and better than
Fearful spoils of dangerous man.

In thy fat-jowled deviltry
Friar Tuck shall live in thee;

Thou mayest levy tithe and dole;
   Thou shalt spread the woodland cheer,
From the pilgrim taking toll;
   Match thy cunning with his fear;
Eat, and drink, and have thy fill;
Yet remain an outlaw still!

NATURE

By Jones Very

THE bubbling brook doth leap
    when I come by,
Because my feet find measure
    with its call;
The birds know when the friend
    they love is nigh,
For I am known to them, both
    great and small.
The flower that on the lonely hillside grows
Expects me there when Spring its bloom has given;
And many a tree and bush my wandering knows,
And e'en the clouds and silent stars of heaven;
For he who with his Maker walks aright,
Shall be their lord as ADAM was before;
His ear shall catch each sound with new delight,
Each object wear the dress that then it wore;
And he, as when erect in soul he stood,
Hear from his Father's lips that all is good.

SEEKING THE MAY-FLOWER

By Edmund Clarence Stedman

HE sweetest sound our whole
 year round —
  'Tis the first robin of the
  spring!
The song of the full orchard
 choir
  Is not so fine a thing.

Glad sights are common: Nature draws
 Her random pictures through the year,
But oft her music bids us long
 Remember those most dear.

To me, when in the sudden spring
 I hear the earliest robin's lay,
With the first trill there comes again
 One picture of the May.

The veil is parted wide, and lo,
 A moment, though my eyelids close,
Once more I see that wooded hill
 Where the arbutus grows.

I see the village dryad kneel,
 Trailing her slender fingers through
The knotted tendrils, as she lifts
 Their pink, pale flowers to view.

Once more I dare to stoop beside
  The dove-eyed beauty of my choice,
And long to touch her careless hair,
  And think how dear her voice.

My eager, wandering hands assist
  With fragrant blooms her lap to fill,
And half by chance they meet her own,
  Half by our young hearts' will.

Till, at the last, those blossoms won, —
  Like her, so pure, so sweet, so shy, —
Upon the gray and lichened rocks
  Close at her feet I lie.

Fresh blows the breeze through hemlock trees,
  The fields are edged with green below;
And naught but youth and hope and love
  We know or care to know!

Hark! from the moss-clung apple-bough,
  Beyond the tumbled wall, there broke
That gurgling music of the May, —
  'Twas the first robin spoke!

I heard it, ay, and heard it not, —
  For little then my glad heart wist
What toil and time should come to pass,
  And what delight be missed;

Nor thought thereafter, year by year,
  Hearing that fresh yet olden song,
To yearn for unreturning joys
  That with its joy belong.

WHAT THE WINDS BRING

By Edmund Clarence Stedman

WHICH is the wind that brings the
cold?
The north-wind, Freddy, and
all the snow;
And the sheep will scamper into
the fold
When the north begins to blow.

Which is the wind that brings the heat?
The south-wind, Katy; and corn will grow,
And peaches redden for you to eat,
When the south begins to blow.

Which is the wind that brings the rain?
The east-wind, Arty; and farmers know
That cows come shivering up the lane
When the east begins to blow.

Which is the wind that brings the flowers?
The west-wind, Bessy; and soft and low
The birdies sing in the summer hours
When the west begins to blow.

UNDER THE LEAVES

By Albert Laighton

OFT have I walked these woodland paths,
Without the blessed foreknowing
That underneath the withered leaves
The fairest buds were growing.

To-day the south-wind sweeps away
  The types of autumn's splendor,
And shows the sweet arbutus flowers, —
  Spring's children, pure and tender.

O prophet-flowers! — with lips of bloom,
  Outvying in your beauty
The pearly tints of ocean shells, —
  Ye teach me faith and duty!

Walk life's dark ways, ye seem to say,
  With love's divine foreknowing,
That where man sees but withered leaves,
  God sees sweet flowers growing.

NANTASKET

By Mary Clemmer Ames

(From " Nantasket ")

FAIR is thy face, Nantasket,
  And fair thy curving shores;
The peering spires of villages;
  The boatman's dipping oars;
The lonely ledge of Minot,
  Where the watchman tends
    his light,
And sets its perilous beacon —
  A star in the stormiest night.

Along thy vast sea highways
  The great ships slide from sight,
And flocks of wingèd phantoms
  Flit by like birds in flight.

Over the toppling sea-wall
  The homebound dories float;
I see the patient fisherman
  Bend in his anchored boat.

I am alone with Nature,
  With the soft September day;
The lifting hills above me,
  With golden-rod are gay.
Across the fields of ether
  Flit butterflies at play;
And cones of garnet sumach
  Glow down the country way.

The autumn dandelion
  Beside the roadside burns;
Above the lichened bowlders
  Quiver the plumèd ferns.
The cream-white silk of the milkweed
  Floats from its sea-green pod;
From out the mossy rock-seams
  Flashes the golden-rod.

The woodbine's scarlet banners
  Flaunt from their towers of stone;
The wan, wild morning-glory
  Dies by the road alone.
By the hill-path to the seaside
  Wave myriad azure bells;
Over the grassy ramparts
  Bend milky immortelles.

I see the tall reeds shiver
  Beside the salt sea marge;
I see the seabird glimmer
  Far out on airy barge.
The cumulate cry of the cricket
  Pierces the amber noon;
Over and through it Ocean
  Chants his pervasive rune.

Fair is the earth behind me,
  Vast is the sea before;
Afar in the misty mirage
  Glistens another shore.
Is it a realm enchanted?
  It cannot be more fair
Than this nook of Nature's kingdom,
  With its spell of space and air.

Lo, over the sapphire ocean
  Trembles a bridge of flame, —
To the burning core of the sunset,
  To the city too fair to name;
Till a ray of its inner glory
  Streams to this lower sea,
And we see with human vision
  What Heaven itself may be.

GREEN THINGS GROWING

By Dinah Mulock Craik

THE green things growing, the green things growing,
The faint sweet smell of the green things growing!
I should like to live, whether I smile or grieve,
Just to watch the happy life of my green things growing.

O the fluttering and the pattering of those green things growing!
How they talk each to each, when none of us are knowing;
In the wonderful white of the weird moonlight
Or the dim dreamy dawn when the cocks are crowing.

I love, I love them so — my green things growing!
And I think that they love me, without false showing;
For by many a tender touch, they comfort me so much,
With the soft mute comfort of green things growing.

And in the rich store of their blossoms glowing
Ten for one I take they're on me bestowing:
Oh, I should like to see, if God's will it may be,
Many, many a summer of my green things growing!

But if I must be gathered for the angel's sowing,
Sleep out of sight awhile, like the green things
    growing,
Though dust to dust return, I think I'll scarcely
    mourn,
If I may change into green things growing.

CORNFIELDS

By Mary Howitt

WHEN on the breath of autumn
    breeze,
    From pastures dry and brown,
Goes floating like an idle thought
    The fair white thistle-down,
O then what joy to walk at will
Upon the golden harvest hill!

What joy in dreamy ease to lie
    Amid a field new shorn,
And see all round on sun-lit slopes
    The piled-up stacks of corn;
And send the fancy wandering o'er
All pleasant harvest-fields of yore.

I feel the day — I see the field,
    The quivering of the leaves,
And good old Jacob and his house
    Binding the yellow sheaves;
And at this very hour I seem
To be with Joseph in his dream.

I see the fields of Bethlehem,
   And reapers many a one,
Bending unto their sickles' stroke —
   And Boaz looking on ;
And Ruth, the Moabite so fair,
Among the gleaners stooping there.

Again I see a little child,
   His mother's sole delight, —
God's living gift unto
   The kind, good Shunamite ;
To mortal pangs I see him yield,
And the lad bear him from the field.

The sun-bathed quiet of the hills,
   The fields of Galilee,
That eighteen hundred years ago
   Were full of corn, I see ;
And the dear Saviour takes his way
'Mid ripe ears on the Sabbath day.

O golden fields of bending corn,
   How beautiful they seem !
The reaper-folk, the piled-up sheaves,
   To me are like a dream.
The sunshine and the very air
Seem of old time, and take me there.

AUGUST

By Celia Thaxter

UTTERCUP nodded and said good-by,
　Clover and daisy went off together,
But the fragrant water-lilies lie
　Yet moored in the golden August weather.
The swallows chatter about their flight,
　The cricket chirps like a rare good fellow,
The asters twinkle in clusters bright,
　While the corn grows ripe and the apples mellow.

WILD GEESE

By Celia Thaxter

HE wind blows, the sun shines, the birds sing loud,
　The blue, blue sky is flecked with fleecy dappled cloud,
　Over earth's rejoicing fields the children dance and sing,
　And the frogs pipe in chorus, "It is spring! It is spring!"

The grass comes, the flower laughs where lately lay the snow,
O'er the breezy hill-top hoarsely calls the crow,

By the flowing river the alder catkins swing,
And the sweet song-sparrow cries, " Spring! It is
    spring! "

Hark, what a clamor goes winging through the sky!
Look, children! Listen to the sound so wild and
    high!
Like a peal of broken bells, — kling, klang, kling, —
Far and high the wild geese cry, " Spring! It is
    spring! "

Bear the winter off with you, O wild geese dear!
Carry all the cold away, far away from here ;
Chase the snow into the north, O strong of heart
    and wing,
While we share the robin's rapture, crying, " Spring!
    It is spring! "

THE SANDPIPER

By Celia Thaxter

CROSS the narrow beach we flit,
    One little sandpiper and I,
And fast I gather, bit by bit,
    The scattered d r i f t w o o d
      bleached and dry.
    The wild waves reach their
      hands for it,
  The wild wind raves, the tide runs high,
As up and down the beach we flit, —
    One little sandpiper and I.

Above our heads the sullen clouds
　Scud black and swift across the sky;
Like silent ghosts in misty shrouds
　Stand out the white lighthouses high.
Almost as far as eye can reach
　I see the close-reefed vessels fly,
As fast we flit along the beach,—
　One little sandpiper and I.

I watch him as he skims along,
　Uttering his sweet and mournful cry.
He starts not at my fitful song,
　Or flash of fluttering drapery.
He has no thought of any wrong;
　He scans me with a fearless eye.
Stanch friends are we, well tried and strong,
　The little sandpiper and I.

Comrade, where wilt thou be to-night
　When the loosed storm breaks furiously?
My driftwood fire will burn so bright!
　To what warm shelter canst thou fly?
I do not fear for thee, though wroth
　The tempest rushes through the sky:
For are we not God's children both,
　Thou, little sandpiper and I?

THE BIRDS OF SCOTLAND

By Hugh Macdonald

THE birds of bonnie Scotland,
  I love them one and all —
The eagle soaring high in pride,
  The wren so blithe and small.
I love the cushat in the wood,
  The heron by the stream,
The lark that sings the stars
    asleep,
The merle that wakes their beam.

O the birds of dear old Scotland,
  I love them every one —
The owl that leaves the tower by night,
  The swallow in the sun.
I love the raven on the rock,
  The sea-bird on the shore,
The merry chaffinch in the wood,
  And the curlew on the moor.

O the birds of bonnie Scotland,
  How lovely are they all!
The oozel by the forest spring
  Or lonely waterfall!
The thrush that from the leafless bough
  Delights the infant year,
The redbreast wailing sad and lone,
  When leaves are falling sear.

O for the time when first I roamed
   The woodland and the field,
A silent sharer in the joy
   Each summer minstrel pealed.
Their nests I knew them every one —
   In bank, or bush, or tree;
Familiar as a voice of home,
   Their every tone of glee.

They tell of birds in other climes
   In richest plumage gay,
With gorgeous tints that far outshine
   An eastern king's array.
Strangers to song! more dear to me
   The linnet, modest gray,
That pipes among the yellow broom
   His wild, heart-witching lay.

More dear than all their shining hues,
   The wells of glee that lie
In throstle's matchless mottled breast
   Or merle's of ebon dye.
And though a lordling's wealth were mine,
   In some far sunny spot,
My heart could never own a home
   Where minstrel birds were not.

Sweet wilding birds of Scotland,
   I loved ye when a boy,
And to my soul your names are linked
   With dreams of vanished joy.
And I could wish, when death's cold hand

Has stilled this heart of mine,
That o'er my last low bed of earth
Might swell your notes divine.

TO AN ORIOLE

By Edgar Fawcett

HOW falls it, oriole, thou hast
    come to fly
In tropic splendor through our
    Northern sky?

At some glad moment was it
    nature's choice
To dower a scrap of sunset with
    a voice?

Or did some orange tulip, flaked with black,
In some forgotten garden, ages back,

Yearning toward Heaven until its wish was heard,
Desire unspeakably to be a bird?

A TOAD

By Edgar Fawcett

BLUE dusk, that brings the dewy hours,
    Brings thee, of graceless form in sooth,
Dark stumbler at the roots of flowers,
    Flaccid, inert, uncouth.

Right ill can human wonder guess
　　Thy meaning or thy mission here,
Gray lump of mottled clamminess,
　　With that preposterous leer!

But when I meet thy dull bulk where
　　Luxurious roses bend and burn,
Or some slim lily lifts to air
　　Its frail and fragrant urn,

Of these, among the garden-ways,
　　So grim a watcher dost thou seem,
That I, with meditative gaze,
　　Look down on thee and dream

Of thick-lipped slaves, with ebon skin,
　　That squat in hideous dumb repose,
And guard the drowsy ladies in
　　Their still seraglios!

A WHITE CAMELLIA

By Edgar Fawcett

IMPERIAL bloom, whose every curve we see
　　So glacial a symmetry control,
Looking, in your pale odorless apathy,
　　Like the one earthly flower that has no soul,

With all sweet radiance bathed in chill eclipse,
　　Pure shape of colorless majesty, you seem
The rose that silence first laid on her lips,
　　Far back among the shadowy days of dream!

By such inviolate calmness you are girt,
  I doubt, while wondering at the spell it weaves,
If even decay's dark hand shall dare to hurt
  The marble immobility of your leaves!

For never sunbeam yet had power to melt
  This virginal coldness, absolute as though
Diana's awful chastity still dwelt
  Regenerate amid your blossoming snow.

And while my silent reverie deeply notes
  What arctic torpor in your bosom lies,
A wandering thought across my spirit floats,
  Like a new bird along familiar skies.

White ghost, in centuries past, has dread mischance
  Thus ruined your vivid warmth, your fragrant
    breath,
While making you, by merciless ordinance,
  The first of living flowers that gazed on death?

THE HUMMING-BIRD

By John Banister Tabb

A FLASH of harmless lightning,
  A mist of rainbow dyes,
  The burnished sunbeams brightening,
  From flower to flower he flies:

While wakes the nodding blossom,
  But just too late to see
What lip hath touched her bosom
  And drained her nectary.

THE WATER-LILY

By John Banister Tabb

WHENCE, O fragrant form of light,
    Hast thou drifted through the night,
    Swanlike, to a leafy nest,
    On the restless waves, at rest?

Art thou from the snowy zone
Of a mountain-summit blown,
Or the blossom of a dream,
Fashioned in the foamy stream?

Nay; methinks the maiden moon,
When the daylight came too soon,
Fleeting from her bath to hide,
Left her garment in the tide.

THE SONG-SPARROW

By Henry van Dyke

THERE is a bird I know so well,
    It seems as if he must have sung
    Beside my crib when I was young;
Before I knew the way to spell
    The name of even the smallest bird,
    His gentle-joyful song I heard.

Now see if you can tell, my dear,
What bird it is that, every year,
Sings " *Sweet — sweet — sweet — very merry cheer.*"

He comes in March, when winds are strong,
 And snow returns to hide the earth ;
 But still he warms his heart with mirth,
And waits for May. He lingers long
 While flowers fade ; and every day
 Repeats his small, contented lay ;
As if to say, we need not fear
The season's change, if love is here
With " *Sweet — sweet — sweet — very merry cheer.*"

He does not wear a Joseph's-coat
 Of many colors, smart and gay ;
 His suit is Quaker brown and gray,
With darker patches at his throat.
 And yet of all the well-dressed throng
 Not one can sing so brave a song.
It makes the pride of looks appear
A vain and foolish thing, to hear
His " *Sweet — sweet — sweet — very merry cheer.*"

A lofty place he does not love,
 But sits by choice, and well at ease,
 In hedges, and in little trees
That stretch their slender arms above
 The meadow-brook ; and there he sings
 Till all the field with pleasure rings ;
And so he tells in every ear,
That lowly homes to heaven are near
In " *Sweet — sweet — sweet — very merry cheer.*"

I like the tune, I like the words;
   They seem so true, so free from art,
   So friendly, and so full of heart,
That if but one of all the birds
   Could be my comrade everywhere,
   My little brother of the air,
This is the one I'd choose, my dear,
Because he'd bless me, every year,
With " *Sweet — sweet — sweet — very merry cheer.*"

AN ANGLER'S WISH

By Henry van Dyke

I

WHEN tulips bloom in Union
   Square,
And timid breaths of vernal air
   Go wandering down the dusty
     town,
   Like children lost in Vanity
     Fair;

When every long, unlovely row
Of westward houses stands aglow,
   And leads the eyes toward sunset skies
Beyond the hills where green trees grow;

Then weary seems the street parade,
And weary books, and weary trade:
   I'm only wishing to go a-fishing;
For this the month of May was made.

II

I guess the pussy-willows now
Are creeping out on every bough
   Along the brook; and robins look
For early worms behind the plough.

The thistle-birds have changed their dun,
For yellow coats, to match the sun;
   And in the same array of flame
The Dandelion Show 's begun.

The flocks of young anemones
Are dancing round the budding trees :
   Who can help wishing to go a-fishing
In days as full of joy as these ?

III

I think the meadow-lark's clear sound
Leaks upward slowly from the ground,
   While on the wing the blue-birds ring
Their wedding-bells to woods around.

The flirting chewink calls his dear
Behind the bush; and very near,
   Where water flows, where green grass grows,
Song-sparrows gently sing, " Good cheer."

And, best of all, through twilight's calm
The hermit-thrush repeats his psalm.
   How much I'm wishing to go a-fishing
In days so sweet with music's balm !

IV

'T is not a proud desire of mine;
I ask for nothing superfine;
   No heavy weight, no salmon great,
To break the record — or my line :

Only an idle little stream,
Whose amber waters softly gleam,
   Where I may wade, through woodland shade,
And cast the fly, and loaf, and dream :

Only a trout or two, to dart
From foaming pools, and try my art :
   No more I'm wishing — old-fashioned fishing,
And just a day on Nature's heart.

DAWN

By Richard Watson Gilder

HE night was dark, though sometimes a faint star
A little while a little space made bright.
Dark was the night and like an iron bar
Lay heavy on the land — till o'er the sea
Slowly, within the East, there grew a light
Which half was starlight, and half seemed to be
The herald of a greater. The pale white
Turned slowly to pale rose, and up the height

Of heaven slowly climbed.   The gray sea grew
Rose-colored like the sky.   A white gull flew
Straight toward the utmost boundary of the East
Where slowly the rose gathered and increased.
There was light now, where all was black before.
It was as on the opening of a door
By one who in his hand a lamp doth hold,
(Its flame being hidden by the garment's fold) —
The still air moves, the wide room is less dim.
>>More bright the East became, the ocean
>>>turned
Dark and more dark against the brightening sky —
Sharper against the sky the long sea line.
The hollows of the breakers on the shore
Were green like leaves whereon no sun doth shine,
Though sunlight make the outer branches hoar.
From rose to red the level heaven burned;
Then sudden, as if a sword fell from on high,
A blade of gold flashed on the ocean's rim.

THE VOICE OF THE PINE

By Richard Watson Gilder

'TIS night upon the lake. Our bed of
boughs
Is built where, high above, the pine-tree
soughs.
'Tis still — and yet what woody noises loom
Against the background of the silent gloom !
One well might hear the opening of a flower
If day were hushed as this.   A mimic shower

Just shaken from a branch, how large it sounded,
As 'gainst our canvas roof its three drops bounded!
Across the rumpling waves the hoot-owl's bark
Tolls forth the midnight hour upon the dark.
What mellow booming from hills doth come? —
The mountain quarry strikes its mighty drum.

Long had we lain beside our pine-wood fire,
From things of sport our talk had risen higher.
How frank and intimate the words of men
When tented lonely in some forest glen!
No dallying now with masks, from whence emerges
Scarce one true feature forth. The night-wind
    urges
To straight and simple speech. So we had thought
Aloud; no secrets but to light were brought.
The hid and spiritual hopes, the wild,
Unreasoned longings that, from child to child,
Mortals still cherish (though with modern shame)—
To these, and things like these, we gave a name;
And as we talked, the intense and resinous fire
Lit up the towering boles, till nigh and nigher
They gather round, a ghostly company,
Like beasts who seek to know what men may be.

Then to our hemlock beds, but not to sleep —
For listening to the stealthy steps that creep
About the tent, or falling branch, but most
A noise was like the rustling of a host,
Or like the sea that breaks upon the shore —
It was the pine-tree's murmur. More and more
It took a human sound. These words I felt
Into the skyey darkness float and melt:

" Heardst thou these wanderers reasoning of a
time
When men more near the Eternal One shall climb ?
How like the new-born child, who cannot tell
A mother's arm that wraps it warm and well !
Leaves of His rose; drops in His sea that flow, —
Are they, alas, so blind they may not know
Here, in this breathing world of joy and fear,
They can no nearer get to God than here."

A SONG OF EARLY AUTUMN
By Richard Watson Gilder

WHEN late in summer the streams
run yellow,
Burst the bridges and spread
into bays ;
When berries are black and
peaches are mellow,
And hills are hidden by rainy
haze ;

When the goldenrod is golden still,
But the heart of the sunflower is darker and
sadder ;
When the corn is in stacks on the slope of the hill,
And slides o'er the path the stripèd adder.

When butterflies flutter from clover to thicket,
Or wave their wings on the drooping leaf ;
When the breeze comes shrill with the call of the
cricket,
Grasshopper's rasp, and rustle of sheaf.

When high in the field the fern-leaves wrinkle,
 And brown is the grass where the mowers have
  mown;
When low in the meadow the cow-bells tinkle,
 And small brooks crinkle o'er stock and stone.

When heavy and hollow the robin's whistle
 And shadows are deep in the heat of noon;
When the air is white with the down o' the thistle,
 And the sky is red with the harvest moon;

Oh then be chary, young Robert and Mary,
 No time let slip, not a moment wait!
  If the fiddle would play it must stop its tuning,
  And they who would wed must be done
   with their mooning;
Let the churn rattle, see well to the cattle,
 And pile the wood by the barn-yard gate!

"GREAT NATURE IS AN ARMY GAY"

By Richard Watson Gilder

GREAT nature is an army gay,
 Resistless marching on its way;
 I hear the bugles clear and sweet,
I hear the tread of million feet.
 Across the plain I see it pour;
It tramples down the waving grass;
Within the echoing mountain-pass
 I hear a thousand cannon roar.

It swarms within my garden gate;
My deepest well it drinketh dry.
It doth not rest; it doth not wait;
By night and day it sweepeth by;
Ceaseless it marches by my door;
It heeds me not, though I implore.
I know not whence it comes, nor where
It goes. For me it doth not care —
Whether I starve, or eat, or sleep,
Or live, or die, or sing, or weep.
And now the banners all are bright,
Now torn and blackened by the fight.
Sometimes its laughter shakes the sky,
Sometimes the groans of those who die.
Still through the night and through the livelong day
The infinite army marches on its remorseless way.

DECEMBER

By Joel Benton

WHEN the feud of hot and cold
        Leaves the autumn woodlands
            bare;
When the year is getting old,
        And flowers are dead, and keen
            the air;

When the crow has new concern,
        And early sounds his raucous note;
And — where the late witch-hazels burn —
        The squirrel from a chuckling throat

Tells that one larder's space is filled,
    And tilts upon a towering tree;
And, valiant, quick, and keenly thrilled,
    Upstarts the tiny chickadee;

When the sun's still shortening arc
    Too soon night's shadows dun and gray
Brings on, and fields are drear and dark,
    And summer birds have flown away, —

I feel the year's slow-beating heart,
    The sky's chill prophecy I know;
And welcome the consummate art
    Which weaves this spotless shroud of snow!

IN JUNE

By Nora Perry

SO sweet, so sweet the roses in
        their blowing,
    So sweet the daffodils, so fair
        to see;
So blithe and gay the humming-
        bird a-going
    From flower to flower, a-hunt-
        ing with the bee.

So sweet, so sweet the calling of the thrushes,
    The calling, cooing, wooing, everywhere;
So sweet the water's song through reeds and rushes,
    The plover's piping note, now here, now there.

So sweet, so sweet from off the fields of clover
  The west wind blowing, blowing up the hill;
So sweet, so sweet with news of some one's lover,
  Fleet footsteps, ringing nearer, nearer still.

So near, so near, now listen, listen thrushes;
  Now plover, blackbird, cease, and let me hear;
And water, hush your song through reeds and
    rushes
  That I may know whose lover cometh near.

So loud, so loud the thrushes kept their calling,
  Plover or blackbird never heeding me;
So loud the mill-stream too kept fretting, falling,
  O'er bar and bank, in brawling, boisterous
    glee.

So loud, so loud; yet blackbird, thrush, nor
    plover,
  Nor noisy mill-stream, in its fret and fall,
Could drown the voice, the low voice of my
    lover,
  My lover calling through the thrushes' call.

" Come down, come down ! " he called, and straight
    the thrushes
  From mate to mate sang all at once, " Come
    down ! "
And while the water laughed through reeds and
    rushes,
  The blackbird chirped, the plover piped, " Come
    down ! "

Then down and off, and through the fields of
    clover,
  I followed, followed, at my lover's call;
Listening no more to blackbird, thrush, or plover,
    The water's laugh, the mill-stream's fret and fall.

AUGUST

By William Davis Gallagher

DUST on my mantle! dust,
  Bright Summer, on thy livery of
    green!
  A tarnish, as of rust,
    Dims thy late-brilliant sheen:
And thy young glories — leaf,
    and bud, and flower —
Change cometh over them with every hour.

  Thee hath the August sun
Looked on with hot, and fierce, and brassy face:
  And still and lazily run,
    Scarce whispering in their pace,
The half-dried rivulets, that lately sent
A shout of gladness up, as on they went.

  Flame-like, the long mid-day —
With not so much of sweet air as hath stirr'd
  The down upon the spray,
    Where rests the panting bird,
Dozing away the hot and tedious noon,
With fitful twitter, sadly out of tune.

Seeds in the sultry air,
And gossamer web-work on the sleeping trees!
  E'en the tall pines, that rear
  Their plumes to catch the breeze,
The slightest breeze from the unrefreshing west,
Partake the general languor, and deep rest.

  Happy, as man can be,
Stretch'd on his back, in homely bean-vine bower,
  While the voluptuous bee
  Robs each surrounding flower,
And prattling childhood clambers o'er his breast,
The husbandman enjoys his noon-day rest.

  Against the hazy sky
The thin and fleecy clouds, unmoving, rest.
  Beneath them far, yet high
  In the dim, distant west,
The vulture, scenting thence its carrion-fare,
Sails, slowly circling in the sunny air.

  Soberly, in the shade,
Repose the patient cow, and toil-worn ox;
  Or in the shoal stream wade,
  Sheltered by jutting rocks:
The fleecy flock, fly-scourg'd and restless, rush
Madly from fence to fence, from bush to bush.

  Tediously pass the hours,
And vegetation wilts, with blistered root —
  And droop the thirsting flow'rs,
  Where the slant sunbeams shoot:

But of each tall old tree, the lengthening line,
Slow-creeping eastward, marks the day's decline.

Faster, along the plain,
Moves now the shade, and on the meadow's edge :
The kine are forth again,
The bird flits in the hedge.
Now in the molten west sinks the hot sun.
Welcome, mild eve! — the sultry day is done.

Pleasantly comest thou,
Dew of the evening, to the crisp'd-up grass ;
And the curl'd corn-blades bow,
As the light breezes pass,
That their parch'd lips may feel thee, and expand,
Thou sweet reviver of the fevered land.

So, to the thirsting soul,
Cometh the dew of the Almighty's love ;
And the scathed heart, made whole,
Turneth in joy above,
To where the spirit freely may expand,
And rove, untrammel'd, in that " better land."

THE CARDINAL BIRD

By *William Davis Gallagher*

A DAY and then a week passed by :
The redbird hanging from the sill
Sang not; and all were wondering why
It was so still —
When one bright morning, loud and clear,
Its whistle smote my drowsy ear,

Ten times repeated, till the sound
Filled every echoing niche around;
And all things earliest loved by me, —
The bird, the brook, the flower, the tree, —
Came back again, as thus I heard
    The cardinal bird.

Where maple orchards towered aloft,
    And spicewood bushes spread below,
Where skies were blue, and winds were soft,
    I could but go —
For, opening through a wildering haze,
Appeared my restless childhood's days;
And truant feet and loitering mood
Soon found me in the same old wood
(Illusion's hour but seldom brings
So much the very form of things)
Where first I sought, and saw, and heard
    The cardinal bird.

Then came green meadows, broad and bright,
    Where dandelions, with wealth untold,
Gleamed on the young and eager sight
    Like stars of gold;
And on the very meadow's edge,
Beneath the ragged blackberry hedge,
Mid mosses golden, gray and green,
The fresh young buttercups were seen,
And small spring-beauties, sent to be
The heralds of anemone:
All just as where I earliest heard
    The cardinal bird.

Upon the gray old forest's rim
   I snuffed the crab-tree's sweet perfume;
And farther, where the light was dim,
   I saw the bloom
Of May-apples, beneath the tent
Of umbrel leaves above them bent;
Where oft was shifting light and shade
The blue-eyed ivy wildly strayed;
And Solomon's-seal, in graceful play,
Swung where the straggling sunlight lay:
The same as when I earliest heard
   The cardinal bird.

And on the slope, above the rill
   That wound among the sugar-trees,
I heard them at their labors still,
   The murmuring bees:
Bold foragers! that come and go
Without permit from friend or foe;
In the tall tulip-trees o'erhead
On pollen greedily they fed,
And from low purple phlox, that grew
About my feet, sipped honey-dew: —
How like the scenes when first I heard
   The cardinal bird!

How like! — and yet. . . . The spell grows weak:—
   Ah, but I miss the sunny brow —
The sparkling eye — the ruddy cheek!
   Where, where are now
The three who then beside me stood
Like sunbeams in the dusky wood?

Alas, I am alone! Since then,
They've trod the weary ways of men :
One on the eve of manhood died ;
Two in its flush of power and pride.
Their graves are green, where first we heard
   The cardinal bird.

The redbird, from the window hung,
   Not long my fancies thus beguiled :
Again in maple-groves it sung
   Its wood-notes wild ;
For, rousing with a tearful eye,
I gave it to the trees and sky !
I missed so much those brothers three,
Who walked youth's flowery ways with me,
I could not, dared not but believe
It too had brothers, that would grieve
Till in old haunts again 't was heard, —
   The cardinal bird.

THE ENGLISH SPARROW

By Mary Isabella Forsyth

SO dainty in plumage and hue,
   A study in grey and in brown,
  How little, how little we knew
   The pest he would prove to the town !

From dawn until daylight grows dim,
   Perpetual chatter and scold.
No winter migration for him,
   Not even afraid of the cold !

Scarce a song-bird he fails to molest,
  Belligerent, meddlesome thing!
Wherever he goes as a guest
  He is sure to remain as a King.

Yet, from tip of his tail to his beak,
  I like him, the sociable elf.
The reason is needless to seek, —
  Because I'm a gossip myself.

TO A TROUBLESOME FLY

By *Thomas MacKellar*

 HAT! here again, indomitable
        pest!
      Thou plagu'st me like a pep-
        per-temper'd sprite;
      Thou makest me the butt of
        all thy spite,
And bitest me, and buzzest as in
        jest.
  Ten times I've closed my heavy lids in vain
This early morn to court an hour of sleep;
For thou — tormentor! — constantly dost keep
  Thy whizzing tones resounding through my
    brain,
Or lightest on my sensitive nose, and there
Thou trimm'st thy wings and shak'st thy legs of hair:
  Ten times I've raised my hand in haste to smite,
But thou art off; and ere I lay my head
And fold mine arms in quiet on my bed,
  Thou com'st again — and tak'st another bite.

As Uncle Toby says, " The world is wide
   Enough for thee and me."   Then go, I pray,
   And through this world do take some other way,
And let us travel no more side by side.
   Go, live among the flowers ; go anywhere ;
Or to the empty sugar-hogshead go,
That standeth at the grocer's store below ;
   Go suit thy taste with any thing that's there.
There's his molasses-measure ; there's his cheese,
And ham and herring : — What ! will nothing
     please ?
   Presumptuous imp ! then die ! — But no ! I'll
     smite
Thee not ; for thou, perchance, art young in days,
And rather green as yet in this world's ways ;
   So live and suffer — age may set thee right.

ODE TO AUTUMN

By John Keats

SEASON of mists and mellow
     fruitfulness !
   Close bosom-friend of the
     maturing sun ;
Conspiring with him how to
     load and bless
   With fruit the vines that
     round the thatch-eaves run ;
To bend with apples the mossed cottage-trees,
   And fill all fruit with ripeness to the core ;
    To swell the gourd, and plump the hazel-shells
With a sweet kernel ; to set budding more,

And still more, later flowers for the bees,
Until they think warm days will never cease;
 For Summer has o'erbrimm'd their clammy
  cells.

Who hath not seen thee oft amid thy store?
 Sometimes whoever seeks abroad may find
Thee sitting careless on a granary floor,
 Thy hair soft-lifted by the winnowing wind;
Or on a half-reaped furrow sound asleep,
 Drowsed with the fume of poppies, while thy
  hook
  Spares the next swath and all its twinèd flow-
   ers;
And sometime like a gleaner thou dost keep
 Steady thy laden head across a brook;
 Or by a cider-press, with patient look,
  Thou watchest the last oozings, hours by
   hours.

Where are the songs of spring? Ay, where are
  they?
 Think not of them, thou hast thy music too,—
While barrèd clouds bloom the soft-dying day,
 And touch the stubble-plains with rosy hue;
Then in a wailful choir the small gnats mourn
 Among the river-sallows, borne aloft
  Or sinking as the light wind lives or dies;
And full-grown lambs loud bleat from hilly bourn;
 Hedge-crickets sing, and now with treble soft
 The red-breast whistles from a garden-croft,
  And gathering swallows twitter in the skies.

ODE TO A NIGHTINGALE

By John Keats

Written in the spring of 1819, when suffering
from physical depression, the precursor of his
death, which happened soon after.

Y heart aches, and a drowsy
 numbness pains
 My sense, as though of hem-
  lock I had drunk,
Or emptied some dull opiate to
 the drains
 One minute past, and Lethe-
  ward had sunk :
'Tis not through envy of thy happy lot,
 But being too happy in thy happiness, —
  That thou, light-wingèd Dryad of the trees,
   In some melodious plot
 Of beechen green, and shadows numberless,
  Singest of summer in full-throated ease.

Oh for a draught of vintage, that hath been
 Cooled a long age in the deep-delvèd earth,
Tasting of Flora and the country green,
 Dance, and Provençal song, and sunburnt
  mirth!
Oh for a beaker full of the warm South,

Full of the true, the blushful Hippocrene,
　　With beaded bubbles winking at the brim,
　　　And purple-stainèd mouth;
That I might drink, and leave the world unseen,
　　And with thee fade away into the forest dim:

Fade far away, dissolve, and quite forget
　　What thou among the leaves hast never known,
The weariness, the fever, and the fret
　　　Here, where men sit and hear each other
　　　　groan;
Where palsy shakes a few, sad, last gray hairs;
　　　Where youth grows pale, and specter-thin, and
　　　　dies;
　　　　Where but to think is to be full of sorrow
　　　　And leaden-eyed despairs,
　　Where Beauty cannot keep her lustrous eyes,
　　　　Or new Love pine at them beyond to-
　　　　morrow.

Away! away! for I will fly to thee,
　　Not charioted by Bacchus and his pards,
But on the viewless wings of Poesy,
　　Though the dull brain perplexes and retards:
Already with thee! tender is the night,
　　And haply the Queen-Moon is on her throne,
　　　Clustered around by all her starry Fays;
　　　　But here there is no light,
　　Save what from heaven is with the breezes
　　　blown
　　　　Through verdurous glooms and winding mossy
　　　　ways.

I cannot see what flowers are at my feet,
　Nor what soft incense hangs upon the boughs,
But, in embalmèd darkness, guess each sweet
　Wherewith the seasonable month endows
The grass, the thicket, and the fruit-tree wild ;
　White hawthorn and the pastoral eglantine ;
　　Fast-fading violets, covered up in leaves ;
　　　And mid-May's eldest child,
　The coming musk-rose, full of dewy wine,
　　The murmurous haunt of flies on summer eves.

Darkling I listen ; and, for many a time
　I have been half in love with easeful Death,
Called him soft names in many a musèd rhyme,
　To take into the air my quiet breath ;
Now more than ever seems it rich to die,
　To cease upon the midnight with no pain,
　　While thou art pouring forth thy soul abroad
　　　In such an ecstasy !
　Still wouldst thou sing, and I have ears in vain, —
　　To thy high requiem become a sod.

Thou wast not born for death, immortal Bird !
　No hungry generations tread thee down ;
The voice I hear this passing night was heard
　In ancient days by emperor and clown ;
Perhaps the self-same song that found a path
　Through the sad heart of Ruth, when, sick for
　　　home,
　　She stood in tears amid the alien corn ;
　　　The same that ofttimes hath
　Charmed magic casements opening on the foam
　Of perilous seas, in fairy-lands forlorn.

Forlorn! the very word is like a bell
  To toll me back from thee to my sole self!
Adieu! the Fancy cannot cheat so well
  As she is famed to do, deceiving elf.
Adieu! adieu! thy plaintive anthem fades
    Past the near meadows, over the still stream,
      Up the hill-side; and now 't is buried deep
      In the next valley-glades:
    Was it a vision, or a waking dream?
    Fled is that music:—Do I wake or sleep?

THOUGHTS IN A GARDEN

By *Andrew Marvell*

HOW vainly men themselves amaze,
  To win the palm, the oak, or bays,
And their incessant labors see
Crowned from some single herb or tree,
Whose short and narrow-vergèd shade
Does prudently their toils upbraid;
While all the flowers and trees do close,
To weave the garlands of repose.

  Fair Quiet, have I found thee here,
And Innocence, thy sister dear?
Mistaken long, I sought you then
In busy companies of men.

Your sacred plants, if here below,
Only among the plants will grow :
Society is all but rude
To this delicious solitude.

No white nor red was ever seen
So amorous as this lovely green.
Fond lovers, cruel as their flame,
Cut in these trees their mistress' name :
Little, alas ! they know or heed
How far these beauties her exceed !
Fair trees ! where'er your barks I wound,
No name shall but your own be found.

When we have run our passion's heat
Love hither makes his best retreat.
The gods, who mortal beauty chase,
Still in a tree did end their race ;
Apollo hunted Daphne so,
Only that she might laurel grow ;
And Pan did after Syrinx speed,
Not as a nymph, but for a reed.

What wondrous life is this I lead !
Ripe apples drop about my head ;
The luscious clusters of the vine
Upon my mouth do crush their wine ;
The nectarine, and curious peach,
Into my hands themselves do reach ;
Stumbling on melons, as I pass,
Ensnared with flowers, I fall on grass.

Meanwhile the mind, from pleasure less,
Withdraws into its happiness, —

The mind, that ocean where each kind
Does straight its own resemblance find,
Yet it creates, transcending these,
Far other worlds, and other seas,
Annihilating all that's made
To a green thought in a green shade.

Here at the fountain's sliding foot,
Or at some fruit-tree's mossy root,
Casting the body's vest aside,
My soul into the boughs does glide;
There, like a bird, it sits and sings,
Then whets and claps its silver wings,
And, till prepared for longer flight,
Waves in its plumes the various light.

Such was that happy garden-state
While man there walk'd without a mate:
After a place so pure and sweet,
What other help could yet be meet!
But 'twas beyond a mortal's share
To wander solitary there:
Two paradises are in one,
To live in Paradise alone.

How well the skilful gardener drew
Of flowers and herbs this dial new
Where, from above, the milder sun
Does through a fragrant zodiac run,
And, as it works, th' industrious bee
Computes its time as well as we!
How could such sweet and wholesome hours
Be reckon'd but with herbs and flowers!

SHADOWS

By *William Sloane Kennedy*

THE moon a light - hung world
    of gold,
Low-drooping, pale, and phan-
    tom-fair;
The fresh pomp of the summer
    leaves,
And fragrance in the breathing
    air.

Beneath the trees flat silhouettes,
Mute idiot shapes that shun the light,
Weird crook-kneed things, a fickle crew,
The restless children of the night.

In idle vacant pantomime
They nod and nod forevermore,
And clutch with aimless fluttering hands,
With thin black hands the leaf-strewn floor.

Quivering, wavering there forever
On the bright and silent ground,
Meshed and tangled there together
While the rolling earth goes round,

And the gold-tinged aery ocean
Ripples light in many a breeze
O'er the sweet-breathed purple lilac,
O'er the tall and slumbering trees.

THE PIPE OF PAN

By Mrs. Elizabeth Akers Allen

HERE in this wild, primeval dell
   Far from the haunts of man,
Where never fashion's footsteps
   fell,
Where shriek of steam nor clang
   of bell,
Nor din of those who buy and
   sell,
Has broken Nature's perfect spell,
May one not hear, who listens well,
   The mystic pipe of Pan?

So virgin and unworldly seem
   All things in this deep glade
Thick curtained from the noonday beam,
That, hearkening, one may almost dream
Fair naiads plashing in the stream,
While graceful limbs and tresses gleam
   Along the dim green shade.

The cool brook runs as clear and sweet
   As ever water ran;
I almost hear the rhythmic beat
Of pattering footfalls, light and fleet,
As Daphne speeds, with flying feet
To hide with leaves her safe retreat, —
   But not the pipe of Pan.

On yonder rocky mountain's sides
   Do oreads dance and climb?
In that dark grot what nymph abides?
And when the freakish wind-god rides,
Do sylphs float on the breezy tides,
While in the hollow tree-trunk hides
   The dryad of old time?

Or is the world so changed to-day
   That all the sylvan clan,
Nymph, dryad, oread, sylph and fay-
Have flown forevermore away,
So, though we watch, and wait, and pray,
Never again on earth will play
   The witching pipe of Pan?

Come, sit on yonder stone and play
   O Pan, thy pipe of reeds,
As when the earth was young and gay,
Long ere this dull and sordid day, —
Play till we learn thy simple lay,
And grief and discord fade away,
   And selfish care recedes!

O, darkened sense! O, dense, deaf ear!
   The world has placed its ban
Against the genii, once so dear,
And strife and greed, for many a year,
Have spoiled the sweet old atmosphere,
So, though he play, we cannot hear
   The wondrous pipe of Pan!

THE MIRACLE-WORKERS

By Mrs. Elizabeth Akers Allen

WHO had seen them, the mystic
sprites,
The working forces of earth
and air,
And light and water, which,
days and nights,
Labor incessantly everywhere?
Those wondrous powers which since the birth
Of growing things, when the first leaf sprung,
Have kept the gracious and fruitful earth
Renewed with years, and forever young.

They taper the sprout to pierce the mould
Of the yielding earth in the early spring,
They edge the columbine's red with gold,
And paint the tanager's brilliant wing,—
They pencil lightly with tender pink
The pale spring-beauty, that hides her flowers
In chilly hollows, where snowdrifts shrink
Under April's persistent showers.

They hang the boughs of the chestnut-tree
With slender tassels of swinging bloom;
They wake the chrysalis tenderly
And call forth life from its winter tomb;
They flatter the strawberry's white to red,
And dint its coral with amber seeds;
They honey the tubes of the clover-heads,
And gild the ear-drops of jewel-weeds.

They trim the lanterns of living light
   That sail the air in the summer eves ;
They stretch the gossamers in the night,
   They curl the tendrils, and notch the leaves.
They lead the bee to the buckwheat-blooms
   Whose hidden nectar he else might miss ;
They deck with garlands of silky plumes
   The clambering length of the clematis.

They weave unseen in some magic loom
   The grass-spread cobwebs, bedropt with light,
And blow to sudden and fragrant bloom
   The evening-primrose buds at night ;
They teach the ox-eyes to dance and swing,
   And top the grass-waves like milk-white
      froth,
They girdle the wasp with a golden ring,
   And powder with silver the candle-moth.

They drape the curtains of morning mist, —
   They bridge with rainbows the cataract's flood,
They prank the pansy, and deftly twist
   The point of the morning-glory bud ;
They give the earthquake its awful force ;
   The dread volcano obeys their word ;
They rouse the whirlwind and shape its course, —
   And bronze the neck of the humming-bird.

They round the dew-drop that winks and shines
   Like a diamond-spark when the grass is wet ;
They trace with purple the dainty lines
   In the cup of the shy white violet ;

They warm the peach with a scarlet streak,
  And touch its velvet with rich perfume;
They redden the ripening apple's cheek,
  And dust the grape with its azure bloom.

They shape the snowflakes in perfect forms
  Of stars and crosses and tiny spheres;
They beckon the tides and rule the storms,
  And rend the rocks of a thousand years, —
But who shall see them, the wondrous powers
  Of earth and water and light and air
Which counting cycles as only hours,
  Labor incessantly everywhere?

SNOW

By Mrs. Elizabeth Akers Allen

O, what wonders the day hath brought,
  Born of the soft and slumbrous snow!
Gradual, silent, slowly wrought;
Even as an artist, thought by thought,
  Writes expression on lip and brow.

Hanging garlands the caves o'erbrim,
  Deep drifts smother the paths below;
The elms are shrouded, trunk and limb,
And all the air is dizzy and dim
  With a whirl of dancing, dazzling snow.

Dimly out of the baffled sight
   Houses and church-spires stretch away;
The trees, all spectral and still and white,
Stand up like ghosts in the failing light,
   And fade and faint with the blinded day.

Down from the roofs in gusts are hurled
   The eddying drifts to the waste below;
And still is the banner of storm unfurled,
Till all the drowned and desolate world
   Lies dumb and white in a trance of snow.

Slowly the shadows gather and fall,
   Still the whispering snow-flakes beat;
Night and darkness are over all:
Rest, pale city, beneath their pall!
   Sleep, white world, in thy winding-sheet!

Clouds may thicken, and storm-winds breathe:
   On my wall is a glimpse of Rome, —
Land of my longing! — and underneath
Swings and trembles my olive-wreath;
   Peace and I are at home, at home!

THE BROOK

By *Alfred Tennyson*

I COME from haunts of coot and hern,
   I make a sudden sally,
And sparkle out among the fern,
To bicker down a valley.

By thirty hills I hurry down,
  Or slip between the ridges,
By twenty thorps, a little town,
  And half a hundred bridges.

Till last by Philip's farm I flow
  To join the brimming river,
For men may come and men may go,
  But I go on for ever.

I chatter over stony ways,
  In little sharps and trebles,
I bubble into eddying bays,
  I babble on the pebbles.

With many a curve my banks I fret
  By many a field and fallow,
And many a fairy foreland set
  With willow-weed and mallow.

I chatter, chatter, as I flow
  To join the brimming river,
For men may come and men may go,
  But I go on for ever.

I wind about, and in and out,
  With here a blossom sailing,
And here and there a lusty trout,
  And here and there a grayling,

And here and there a foamy flake
  Upon me, as I travel
With many a silvery waterbreak
  Above the golden gravel,

And draw them all along, and flow
  To join the brimming river,
For men may come and men may go,
  But I go on for ever.

I steal by lawns and grassy plots,
  I slide by hazel covers;
I move the sweet forget-me-nots
  That grow for happy lovers.

I slip, I slide, I gloom, I glance,
  Among my skimming swallows;
I make the netted sunbeam dance
  Against my sandy shallows.

I murmur under moon and stars
  In brambly wildernesses;
I linger by my shingly bars;
  I loiter round my cresses;

And out again I curve and flow
  To join the brimming river,
For men may come and men may go,
  But I go on for ever.

THE DRAGON-FLY

(From " The Two Voices ")

By Alfred Tennyson

" TO-DAY I saw the dragon-fly
  Come from the wells where he did lie.

  " An inner impulse rent the veil
Of his old husk: from head to tail
Came out clear plates of sapphire mail.

" He dried his wings : like gauze they grew ;
Thro' crofts and pastures wet with dew
A living flash of light he flew."

THE BLACKBIRD

By *Alfred Tennyson*

 BLACKBIRD ! sing me some-
  thing well :
While all the neighbors shoot
  thee round,
I keep smooth plats of fruitful
  ground,
Where thou may'st warble, eat
  and dwell.

The espaliers and the standards all
 Are thine ; the range of lawn and park :
 The unnetted black-hearts ripen dark,
All thine, against the garden wall.

Yet, tho' I spared thee all the spring,
 Thy sole delight is, sitting still,
 With that gold dagger of thy bill
To fret the summer jenneting.

A golden bill ! the silver tongue,
 Cold February loved, is dry :
 Plenty corrupts the melody
That made thee famous once, when young :

And in the sultry garden-squares,
 Now thy flute-notes are changed to coarse,
 I hear thee not at all, or hoarse
As when a hawker hawks his wares.

Take warning! he that will not sing
 While yon sun prospers in the blue,
 Shall sing for want, ere leaves are new,
Caught in the frozen palms of Spring.

A FAREWELL

By Alfred Tennyson

LOW down, cold rivulet, to the
  sea,
  Thy tribute wave deliver:
 No more by thee my steps shall
  be,
  For ever and for ever.

Flow, softly flow, by lawn and lea,
 A rivulet then a river:
No where by thee my steps shall be,
 For ever and for ever.

But here will sigh thine alder tree,
 And here thine aspen shiver;
And here by thee will hum the bee,
 For ever and for ever.

A thousand suns will stream on thee,
A thousand moons will quiver;
But not by thee my steps shall be,
For ever and for ever.

THE EAGLE

(Fragment)

By Alfred Tennyson

 E clasps the crag with hooked
hands;
Close to the sun in lonely lands,
Ring'd with the azure world, he
stands.

The wrinkled sea beneath him
crawls;
He watches from his mountain walls,
And like a thunderbolt he falls.

BREAK, BREAK, BREAK

By Alfred Tennyson

BREAK, break, break,
On thy cold gray stones, O Sea!
And I would that my tongue could utter
The thoughts that arise in me.

O well for the fisherman's boy,
That he shouts with his sister at play!
O well for the sailor lad,
That he sings in his boat on the bay!

And the stately ships go on
   To their haven under the hill;
But O for the touch of a vanish'd hand,
   And the sound of a voice that is still!

Break, break, break,
   At the foot of thy crags, O Sea!
But the tender grace of a day that is dead
   Will never come back to me.

AUTUMN

(From " In Memoriam ")

By Alfred Tennyson

CALM is the morn without a
   sound,
   Calm as to suit a calmer
     grief,
   And only thro' the faded leaf
The chestnut pattering to the
   ground:

Calm and deep peace on this high wold,
   And on these dews that drench the furze,
   And all the silvery gossamers
That twinkle into green and gold:

Calm and still light on yon great plain
   That sweeps with all its autumn bowers,
   And crowded farms and lessening towers,
To mingle with the bounding main:

Calm and deep peace in this wide air,
 These leaves that redden to the fall ;
 And in my heart, if calm at all,
If any calm, a calm despair :

Calm on the seas, and silver sleep,
 And waves that sway themselves in rest,
 And dead calm in that noble breast
Which heaves but with the heaving deep.

THE THROSTLE

By *Alfred Tennyson*

S UMMER is coming, summer
 is coming.
  I know it, I know it, I know
  it.
  Light again, leaf again, life again,
   love again,"
  Yes, my wild little Poet.

Sing the new year in under the blue.
 Last year you sang it as gladly.
" New, new, new, new ! " Is it then *so* new
 That you should carol so madly ?

" Love again, song again, nest again, young again,"
 Never a prophet so crazy !
And hardly a daisy as yet, little friend,
 See, there is hardly a daisy.

"Here again, here, here, here, happy year!
  O warble unchidden, unbidden!
Summer is coming, is coming, my dear,
  And all the winters are hidden."

APRIL DAYS

(From "In Memoriam")

By Alfred Tennyson

IP down upon the northern shore,
  O sweet new-year delaying long;
  Thou doest expectant nature wrong;
Delaying long, delay no more.

What stays thee from the clouded noons,
  Thy sweetness from its proper place?
  Can trouble live with April days,
Or sadness in the summer moons?

Bring orchis, bring the foxglove spire,
  The little speedwell's darling blue,
  Deep tulips dash'd with fiery dew,
Laburnums, dropping-wells of fire.

O thou, new-year, delaying long,
  Delayest the sorrow in my blood,
  That longs to burst a frozen bud,
And flood a fresher throat with song.

EARLY SPRING

By *Alfred Tennyson*

I

ONCE more the Heavenly Power
    Makes all things new,
And domes the red-plow'd hills
    With loving blue;
The blackbirds have their wills,
    The throstles too.

II

Opens a door in Heaven;
    From skies of glass
A Jacob's ladder falls
    On greening grass,
And o'er the mountain-walls
    Young angels pass.

III

Before them fleets the shower,
    And burst the buds,
And shine the level lands,
    And flash the floods;
The stars are from their hands
    Flung thro' the woods,

IV

The woods with living airs
   How softly fann'd,
Light airs from where the deep,
   All down the sand,
Is breathing in his sleep,
   Heard by the land.

V

O follow, leaping blood,
   The season's lure!
O heart, look down and up,
   Serene, secure,
Warm as the crocus cup,
   Like snow-drops, pure!

VI

Past, Future glimpse and fade
   Thro' some slight spell,
Some gleam from yonder vale,
   Some far blue fell,
And sympathies, how frail,
   In sound and smell!

VII

Till at thy chuckled note,
   Thou twinkling bird,
The fairy fancies range,
   And, lightly stirred,
Ring little bells of change
   From word to word.

VIII

For now the Heavenly Power
Makes all things new,
And thaws the cold, and fills
The flower with dew;
The blackbirds have their wills,
The poets too.

SPRING

(From " In Memoriam ")

By Alfred Tennyson

OW fades the last long streak of
snow,
Now burgeons every maze of
quick
About the flowering squares,
and thick
By ashen roots the violets blow.

Now rings the woodland loud and long,
The distance takes a lovelier hue,
And drown'd in yonder living blue
The lark becomes a sightless song.

Now dance the lights on lawn and lea,
The flocks are whiter down the vale,
And milkier every milky sail
On winding stream or distant sea;

Where now the seamew pipes, or dives
   In yonder greening gleam, and fly
   The happy birds, that change their sky
To build and brood; that live their lives

From land to land; and in my breast
   Spring wakens too; and my regret
   Becomes an April violet,
And buds, and blossoms like the rest.

THE SHELL

(From " Maud ")

By Alfred Tennyson

I

SEE what a lovely shell,
   Small and pure as a pearl,
   Lying close to my foot,
   Frail, but a work divine,
Made so fairly well
   With delicate spire and whorl,
   How exquisitely minute,
   A miracle of design!

II

What is it? a learned man
Could give it a clumsy name.
Let him name it who can,
The beauty would be the same.

III

The tiny cell is forlorn,
Void of the little living will
That made it stir on the shore.
Did he stand at the diamond door
Of his house in a rainbow frill?
Did he push, when he was uncurl'd,
A golden foot or a fairy horn
Thro' his dim water-world?

IV

Slight, to be crush'd with a tap
Of my finger-nail on the sand,
Small, but a work divine,
Frail, but of force to withstand,
Year upon year, the shock
Of cataract seas that snap
The three decker's oaken spine
Athwart the ledges of rock,
Here on the Breton strand!

"I AM AN ACME OF THINGS ACCOMPLISHED"

(From " Walt Whitman ")

By *Walt Whitman*

I AM an acme of things accomplished, and I an encloser of things to be.

My feet strike an apex of the apices of the stairs;

On every step bunches of ages, and larger bunches
    between the steps;
All below duly travell'd, and still I mount and
    mount.

Rise after rise bow the phantoms behind me;
Afar down I see the huge first Nothing — I know
    I was even there;
I waited unseen and always, and slept through the
    lethargic mist,
And took my time, and took no hurt from the fetid
    carbon.

Long I was hugg'd close — long and long.

Immense have been the preparations for me,
Faithful and friendly the arms that have help'd me.

Cycles ferried my cradle, rowing and rowing like
    cheerful boatmen;
For room to me stars kept aside in their own rings;
They sent influences to look after what was to
    hold me.

Before I was born out of my mother, generations
    guided me.
My embryo has never been torpid — nothing could
    overlay it.

For it the nebula cohered to an orb,
The long slow strata piled to rest it on,
Vast vegetables gave it sustenance,
Monstrous sauroids transported it in their mouths,
    and deposited it with care.

All forces have been steadily employ'd to complete
    and delight me ;
Now on this spot I stand with my robust Soul.

THE MICROCOSM

(From " Walt Whitman ")

By *Walt Whitman*

 BELIEVE a leaf of grass is no
less than the journey-work
of the stars,
And the pismire is equally per-
fect, and a grain of sand,
and the egg of the wren,
And the tree-toad is a chef-
d'œuvre for the highest,
And the running blackberry would adorn the parlors
of heaven,
And the narrowest hinge in my hand puts to scorn
all machinery,
And the cow crunching with depress'd head sur-
passes any statue,
And a mouse is miracle enough to stagger sextil-
lions of infidels,
And I could come every afternoon of my life to
look at the farmer's girl boiling her iron tea-
kettle and baking short-cake.

I find I incorporate gneiss, coal, long-threaded moss,
    fruits, grains, esculent roots,
And am stucco'd with quadrupeds and birds all
    over,
And have distanced what is behind me for good
    reasons,
And call anything close again, when I desire it.

In vain the speeding or shyness;
In vain the plutonic rocks send their old heat
    against my approach;
In vain the mastodon retreats beneath its own
    powder'd bones;
In vain objects stand leagues off, and assume mani-
    fold shapes;
In vain the ocean settling in hollows, and the great
    monsters lying low;
In vain the buzzard houses herself with the sky;

In vain the snake slides through the creepers and
    logs;
In vain the elk takes to the inner passes of the
    woods;
In vain the razor-bill'd auk sails far north to Lab-
    rador;
I follow quickly, I ascend to the nest in the fissure
    of the cliff.

"OXEN THAT RATTLE THE YOKE AND CHAIN"

(From " Walt Whitman ")

By Walt Whitman

XEN that rattle the yoke and
    chain, or halt in the leafy
    shade !
What is that you express in
    your eyes ?
It seems to me more than all the
    print I have read in my
    life.

My tread scares the wood-drake and the wood-
    duck, on my distant and day-long ramble ;
They rise together — they slowly circle around.

I believe in those wing'd purposes,
And acknowledge red, yellow, white, playing with-
    in me,
And consider green and violet, and the tufted
    crown, intentional ;
And do not call the tortoise unworthy because she
    is not something else ;
And the jay in the woods never studied the gamut,
    yet trills pretty well to me ;
And the look of the bay mare shames silliness out
    of me.

BARE-BOSOM'D NIGHT

(From " Walt Whitman ")

By Walt Whitman

AM he that walks with the tender and growing night;
I call to the earth and sea, half-held by the night.

Press close, bare-bosom'd night!
Press close, magnetic, nourishing night!
Night of south winds! night of the large few stars!
Still, nodding night! mad, naked, summer night.

Smile, O voluptuous, cool-breath'd earth!
Earth of the slumbering and liquid trees;
Earth of departed sunset! earth of the mountains, misty-topt!

Earth of the vitreous pour of the full moon, just tinged with blue!
Earth of shine and dark, mottling the tide of the river!
Earth of the limpid gray of clouds, brighter and clearer for my sake!
Far-swooping elbow'd earth! rich, apple-blossom'd earth!
Smile, for your lover comes!

Prodigal, you have given me love! Therefore I to you give love!
O unspeakable, passionate love!

YON SEA!

(From " Walt Whitman ")

By *Walt Whitman*

YON sea! I resign myself to you also — I guess what you mean;
I behold from the beach your crooked inviting fingers;
I believe you refuse to go back without feeling of me;
We must have a turn together — I undress — hurry me out of sight of the land;
Cushion me soft, rock me in billowy drowse;
Dash me with amorous wet — I can repay you.

Sea of stretch'd ground-swells!
Sea breathing broad and convulsive breaths!
Sea of the brine of life! sea of unshovell'd yet always-ready graves!
Howler and scooper of storms! capricious and dainty sea!
I am integral with you — I too am of one phase, and of all phases.

THIS COMPOST

(From " Leaves of Grass ")

By *Walt Whitman*

1

SOMETHING startles me where
  I thought I was safest;
I withdraw from the still woods
  I loved;
I will not go now on the past-
  ures to walk;
I will not strip the clothes from
  my body to meet my lover
  the sea;
I will not touch my flesh to the earth, as to other
  flesh, to renew me.

2

O how can it be that the ground itself does not
  sicken?
How can you be alive, you growths of spring?
How can you furnish health, you blood of herbs,
  roots, orchards, grain?
Are they not continually putting distemper'd
  corpses within you?
Is not every continent work'd over and over with
  sour dead?

Where have you disposed of their carcasses?
Those drunkards and gluttons of so many genera-
  tions;

Where have you drawn off all the foul liquid and
    meat ?
I do not see any of it upon you to-day — or per-
    haps I am deceiv'd ;
I will run a furrow with my plough — I will
    press my spade through the sod, and turn it up
    underneath ;
I am sure I shall expose some of the foul meat.

3

Behold this compost ! behold it well !
Perhaps every mite has once form'd part of a sick
    person — Yet behold !
The grass of spring covers the prairies,
The bean bursts noiselessly through the mould in
    the garden,
The delicate spear of the onion pierces upward,
The apple-buds cluster together on the apple-
    branches,
The resurrection of the wheat appears with pale
    visage out of its graves,
The tinge awakes over the willow-tree and the
    mulberry-tree,
The he-birds carol mornings and evenings, while
    the she-birds sit on their nests,
The young of poultry break through the hatched
    eggs,
The new-born of animals appear — the calf is dropt
    from the cow, the colt from the mare,
Out of its little hill faithfully rise the potato's dark
    green leaves,

Out of its hill rises the yellow maize-stalk — the
    lilacs bloom in the door-yards ;
The summer growth is innocent and disdainful
    above all those strata of sour dead.
What chemistry !
That the winds are really not infectious,
That this is no cheat, this transparent green-wash
    of the sea, which is so amorous after me,
That it is safe to allow it to lick my naked body
    all over with its tongues,
That it will not endanger me with the fevers that
    have deposited themselves in it,
That all is clean forever and forever.
That the cool drink from the well tastes so good,
That blackberries are so flavorous and juicy,
That the fruits of the apple-orchard, and of the
    orange-orchard — that melons, grapes, peaches,
    plums, will none of them poison me,
That when I recline on the grass I do not catch
    any disease,
Though probably every spear of grass rises out of
    what was once a catching disease.

4

Now I am terrified at the Earth! it is that calm and
    patient,
It grows such sweet things out of such corruptions,
It turns harmless and stainless on its axis, with
    such endless successions of diseas'd corpses,
It distils such exquisite winds out of such infused
    fetor,

It renews with such unwitting looks, its prodigal,
    annual, sumptuous crops,
It gives such divine materials to men, and accepts
    such leavings from them at last.

THERE WAS A CHILD WENT FORTH

(From " Leaves of Grass ")

By *Walt Whitman*

HERE was a child went forth
    every day ;
And the first object he look'd up-
    on, that object he became ;
And that object became part of
    him for the day, or a certain
    part of the day, or for many
    years, or stretching cycles of
    years.

The early lilacs became part of this child,
And grass, and white and red morning-glories, and
    white and red clover, and the song of the phœbe-
    bird,
And the Third-month lambs, and the sow's pink-
    faint litter, and the mare's foal, and the cow's
    calf,
And the noisy brood of the barn-yard, or by the
    mire of the pond-side,

And the fish suspending themselves so curiously
  below there — and the beautiful curious
  liquid,
And the water-plants with their graceful flat heads
  — all became part of him.

The field-sprouts of Fourth-month and Fifth-
  month became part of him ;
Winter-grain sprouts, and those of the light-yellow
  corn, and the esculent roots of the garden,
And the apple-trees cover'd with blossoms, and
  the fruit afterward, and wood-berries, and the
  commonest weeds by the road ;
And the old drunkard staggering home from the
  out-house of the tavern, whence he had lately
  risen,
And the school-mistress that pass'd on her way to
  the school,
And the friendly boys that pass'd — and the quarrel-
  some boys,
And the tidy and fresh-cheek'd girls — and the
  barefoot negro boy and girl,
And all the changes of city and country, wherever
  he went.

His own parents,
He that had father'd him, and she that had con-
  ceiv'd him in her womb, and birth'd him,
They gave this child more of themselves than
  that ;
They gave him afterward every day — they became
  part of him.

The mother at home, quietly placing the dishes on
the supper-table ;

The mother with mild words — clean her cap and
gown, a wholesome odor falling off her person
and clothes as she walks by ;

The father, strong, self-sufficient, manly, mean,
anger'd, unjust ;

The blow, the quick loud word, the tight bargain,
the crafty lure,

The family usages, the language, the company, the
furniture — the yearning and swelling heart,

Affection that will not be gainsay'd — the sense
of what is real — the thought if, after all, it
should prove unreal,

The doubts of day-time and the doubts of night-
time — the curious whether and how,

Whether that which appears so is so, or is it all
flashes and specks ?

Men and women crowding fast in the streets — if
they are not flashes and specks, what are they ?

The streets themselves, and the façades of houses,
and goods in the windows,

Vehicles, teams, the heavy-plank'd wharves — the
huge crossing at the ferries,

The village on the highland, seen from afar at sun-
set — the river between,

Shadows, aureola and mist, the light falling on
roofs and gables of white or brown, two miles
off,

The schooner near by, sleepily dropping down the
tide — the little boat slack-tow'd astern,

The hurrying tumbling waves, quick-broken crests,
  slapping,
The strata of color'd clouds, the long bar of ma-
  roon-tint, away solitary by itself — the spread
  of purity it lies motionless in,
The horizon's edge, the flying sea-crow, the fra-
  grance of salt marsh and shore mud;
These became part of that child who went forth
  every day, and who now goes, and will always
  go forth every day.

THE CLOSING SCENE

By Thomas Buchanan Read

ITHIN the sober realm of leaf-
  less trees
  The russet year inhaled the
    dreamy air;
Like some tanned reaper in his
  hour of ease,
  When all the fields are lying
    brown and bare.

The gray barns, looking from their hazy hills,
  O'er the dim waters, widening in the vales,
Sent down the air a greeting to the mills,
  On the dull thunder of alternate flails.

All sights were mellowed, and all sounds subdued,
  The hills seemed farther and the streams sang low;
As in a dream, the distant woodman hewed
  His winter log with many a muffled blow.

The embattled forests, erewhile, armed in gold,
  Their banners bright with every martial hue,
Now stood, like some sad beaten host of old
  Withdrawn afar in Time's remotest blue.

On slumberous wings the vulture tried his flight;
  The dove scarce heard his sighing mate's com-
    plaint;
And like a star, slow drowning in the light,
  The village church vane seemed to pale and faint.

The sentinel cock upon the hill-side crew —
  Crew thrice, and all was stiller than before —
Silent till some replying warden blew
  His alien horn, and then was heard no more.

Where, erst, the jay within the elm's tall crest,
  Made garrulous trouble round her unfledged
    young;
And where the oriole hung her swaying nest,
  By every light wind like a censer swung;

Where sang the noisy masons of the eaves,
  The busy swallows circling ever near,
Foreboding, as the rustic mind believes,
  An early harvest, and a plenteous year;

Where every bird that waked the vernal feast
  Shook the sweet slumber from its wings at morn,
To warn the reaper of the rosy east; —
  All now was songless, empty, and forlorn.

Alone, from out the stubble, piped the quail,
  And croaked the crow through all the dreary
    gloom ;
Alone the pheasant, drumming in the vale,
  Made echo to the distant cottage-loom.

There was no bud, no bloom upon the bowers;
  The spiders wove their thin shrouds night by
    night ;
The thistle-down, the only ghost of flowers,
  Sailed slowly by — passed noiseless out of sight.

Amid all this — in this most cheerless air,
  And where the woodbine shed upon the porch
Its crimson leaves, as if the Year stood there,
  Firing the floor with its inverted torch ; —

Amid all this, the centre of the scene,
  The white-haired matron, with monotonous
    tread,
Plied the swift wheel, and with her joyless mien,
  Sat like a fate, and watched the flying thread.

She had known sorrow.   He had walked with her,
  Oft supped, and broke with her the ashen crust,
And, in the dead leaves, still she heard the stir
  Of his black mantle trailing in the dust.

While yet her cheek was bright with summer
    bloom,
  Her country summoned, and she gave her all,
And twice, war bowed to her his sable plume —
  Re-gave the swords, to rust upon the wall.

Re-gave the swords — but not the hand that drew,
  And struck for liberty the dying blow ;
Nor him who, to his sire and country true,
  Fell mid the ranks of the invading foe.

Long, but not loud, the droning wheel went on,
  Like the low murmur of a hive at noon ;
Long, but not loud, the memory of the gone,
  Breathed through her lips a sad and tremulous tune.

At last the thread was snapped — her head was
    bowed ;
  Life dropped the distaff through his hands serene ;
And loving neighbors smoothed her careful shroud,
  While Death and Winter closed the Autumn
    scene.

THE LITTLE BEACH-BIRD

By Richard Henry Dana

THOU little bird, thou dweller by the sea,
    Why takest thou its melancholy voice ?
    Why with that boding cry
  O'er the waves dost thou fly ?
O, rather, bird, with me
  Through the fair land rejoice !

Thy flitting form comes ghostly dim and pale,
  As driven by a beating storm at sea ;
    Thy cry is weak and scared,
    As if thy mates had shared
The doom of us.   Thy wail —
  What does it bring to me ?

Thou call'st along the sand, and haunt'st the surge,
   Restless and sad ; as if, in strange accord
     With the motion, and the roar
   Of waves that drive to shore,
One spirit did ye urge —
   The Mystery — the Word.

Of thousands thou both sepulchre and pall,
   Old ocean, art !   A requiem o'er the dead
     From out thy gloomy cells
   A tale of mourning tells —
Tells of man's woe and fall,
   His sinless glory fled.

Then turn thee, little bird, and take thy flight
   Where the complaining sea shall sadness bring
     Thy spirit never more.
   Come, quit with me the shore
For gladness, and the light
   Where birds of summer sing.

SMOKE

By Henry David Thoreau

LIGHT-WINGED Smoke ! Icarian bird,
   Melting thy pinions in thy upward flight ;
   Lark without song, and messenger of dawn,
Circling above the hamlets as thy nest ;
Or else, departing dream, and shadowy form
Of midnight vision, gathering up thy skirts ;
By night star-veiling, and by day

Darkening the light and blotting out the sun ;
Go thou, my incense, upward from this hearth,
And ask the gods to pardon this clear flame.

MIST

By Henry David Thoreau

OW-ANCHORED cloud,
Newfoundland air,
Fountain-head and source of
    rivers,
Dew-cloth, dream-drapery,
And napkin spread by fays ;
Drifting meadow of the air,
Where bloom the daisied banks and violets,
And in whose fenny labyrinth
The bittern booms and heron wades ;
Spirit of lakes and seas and rivers, —
Bear only perfumes and the scent
Of healing herbs to just men's fields.

THE LARK

By James Hogg

BIRD of the wilderness,
    Blithesome and cumberless,
    Sweet be thy matin o'er moorland and lea !
Emblem of happiness,
    Blest is thy dwelling-place :
O to abide in the desert with thee !

Wild is thy lay, and loud,
Far in the downy cloud;
Love gives it energy — love gave it birth!
Where, on thy dewy wing —
Where art thou journeying?
Thy lay is in heaven, — thy love is on earth.

O'er fell and fountain sheen,
O'er moor and mountain green,
O'er the red streamer that heralds the day;
Over the cloudlet dim,
Over the rainbow's rim,
Musical cherub, soar, singing, away!
Then, when the gloaming comes,
Low in the heather blooms,
Sweet will thy welcome and bed of love be!
Emblem of happiness,
Blest is thy dwelling-place —
O to abide in the desert with thee!

PART OF IL PENSEROSO

By John Milton

SWEET bird, that shunn'st the noise of folly,
Most musical, most melancholy!
Thee, chantress, oft, the woods among,
I woo, to hear thy even-song:
And, missing thee, I walk unseen
On the dry smooth-shaven green,
To behold the wandering moon,
Riding near her highest noon,

Like one that had been led astray
Through the heaven's wide pathless way;
And oft, as if her head she bowed,
Stooping through a fleecy cloud.

PART OF L'ALLEGRO

By John Milton

O hear the lark begin his flight,
And singing startle the dull
night,
From his watch-tower in the
skies,
Till the dappled dawn doth rise;
Then to come in spite of sorrow,
And at my window bid good morrow,
Through the sweet-brier, or the vine,
Or the twisted eglantine;
While the cock with lively din
Scatters the rear of Darkness thin,
And to the stack, or the barn-door,
Stoutly struts his dames before:
Oft listening how the hounds and horn
Cheerly rouse the slumbering Morn,
From the side of some hoar hill
Through the high wood echoing shrill:
Sometime walking, not unseen,
By hedge-row elms, on hillocks green,
Right against the eastern gate,
Where the great sun begins his state,

Robed in flames, and amber light,
The clouds in thousand liveries dight;
While the ploughman near at hand
Whistles o'er the furrowed land,
And the milkmaid singeth blithe,
And the mower whets his scythe,
And every shepherd tells his tale
Under the hawthorn in the dale.
Straight mine eye hath caught new pleasures
Whilst the landscape round it measures;
Russet lawns, and fallows gray,
Where the nibbling flocks do stray, —
Mountains, on whose barren breast
The laboring clouds do often rest, —
Meadows trim with daisies pied,
Shallow brooks, and rivers wide;
Towers and battlements it sees
Bosomed high in tufted trees,
Where perhaps some beauty lies,
The cynosure of neighboring eyes.

THE CRICKET

By William Cowper

LITTLE inmate, full of mirth,
　　Chirping on my kitchen hearth,
　　Whereso'er be thine abode
Always harbinger of good,

Pay me for thy warm retreat
With a song more soft and sweet;
In return thou shalt receive
Such a strain as I can give.

Thus thy praise shall be expressed,
Inoffensive, welcome guest!
While the rat is on the scout,
And the mouse with curious snout,
With what vermin else infest
Every dish, and spoil the best;
Frisking thus before the fire,
Thou hast all thine heart's desire.

Though in voice and shape they be
Formed as if akin to thee,
Thou surpassest, happier far,
Happiest grasshoppers that are;
Theirs is but a summer's song —
Thine endures the winter long,
Unimpaired and shrill, and clear,
Melody throughout the year.

Neither night nor dawn of day
Puts a period to thy play:
Sing then — and extend thy span
Far beyond the date of man;
Wretched man, whose years are spent
In repining discontent,
Lives not, aged though he be,
Half a span, compared with thee.

TO SENECA LAKE

By James Gates Percival

 N thy fair bosom, silver lake,
    The wild swan spreads his
      snowy sail,
And round his breast the ripples
      break,
    As down he bears before the
      gale.

On thy fair bosom, waveless stream,
    The dipping paddle echoes far,
And flashes in the moonlight gleam,
    And bright reflects the polar star.

The waves along thy pebbly shore,
    As blows the north-wind, heave their foam,
And curl around the dashing oar,
    As late the boatman hies him home.

How sweet, at set of sun, to view
    Thy golden mirror spreading wide,
And see the mist of mantling blue
    Float round the distant mountain's side.

At midnight hour, as shines the moon,
    A sheet of silver spreads below,
And swift she cuts, at highest noon,
    Light clouds, like wreaths of purest snow.

On thy fair bosom, silver lake,
  O ! I could ever sweep the oar, —
When early birds at morning wake,
  And evening tells us toil is o'er !

NIGHT AND DEATH

By Joseph Blanco White

YSTERIOUS   Night !   when
     our first parent knew
Thee, from report divine, and
     heard thy name,
Did he not tremble for this lovely
     Frame,
This glorious canopy of Light
     and Blue ?
Yet, 'neath a curtain of translucent dew,
Bathed in the rays of the great setting Flame,
Hesperus, with the Host of Heaven, came,
And lo ! Creation widened on Man's view.
Who could have thought such Darkness lay con-
    cealed
Within thy beams, O Sun ! or who could find,
Whilst flower and leaf and insect stood revealed,
That to such countless Orbs thou mad'st us blind !
Why do we then shun Death with anxious strife ?
If Light can thus deceive, wherefore not Life ?

THE DAISY

By James Montgomery

THERE is a flower, a little flower
With silver crest and golden eye,
That welcomes every changing
    hour,
And weathers every sky.

The prouder beauties of the field,
In gay but quick succession shine;
Race after race their honors yield,
They flourish and decline.

But this small flower, to Nature dear,
While moons and stars their courses run,
Inwreathes the circle of the year
Companion of the sun.

It smiles upon the lap of May,
To sultry August spreads its charm,
Lights pale October on his way,
And twines December's arm.

The purple heath and golden broom,
On moory mountains catch the gale;
O'er lawns the lily sheds perfume,
The violet in the vale.

But this bold floweret climbs the hill,
Hides in the forest, haunts the glen,
Plays on the margin of the rill,
Peeps round the fox's den.

Within the garden's cultured round
It shares the sweet carnation's bed;
And blooms on consecrated ground
In honor of the dead.

The lambkin crops its crimson gem;
The wild bee murmurs on its breast,
The blue-fly bends its pensile stem
Light o'er the skylark's nest.

'Tis Flora's page — in every place,
In every season, fresh and fair;
It opens with perennial grace,
And blossoms everywhere.

On waste and woodland, rock and plain,
Its humble buds unheeded rise;
The rose has but a summer reign;
The Daisy never dies!

THE TIGER

By William Blake

IGER! Tiger! burning bright,
In the forests of the night;
What immortal hand or eye
Could frame thy fearful symme-
try?

In what distant deeps or skies
Burned the fire of thine eyes?
On what wings dare he aspire?
What the hand dare seize the fire?

And what shoulder, and what art,
Could twist the sinews of thine heart?
And when thy heart began to beat,
What dread hand? and what dread feet?

What the hammer, what the chain?
In what furnace was thy brain?
What the anvil? what dread grasp
Dare its deadly terrors clasp?

When the stars threw down their spears,
And watered heaven with their tears,
Did he smile his work to see?
Did He, Who made the Lamb, make thee?

Tiger! Tiger! burning bright,
In the forests of the night,
What immortal hand or eye
Dare frame thy fearful symmetry?

TO THE CUCKOO

By John Logan

HAIL, beauteous stranger of the
grove!
Thou messenger of Spring!
Now heaven repairs thy rural seat,
And woods thy welcome sing.

Soon as the daisy decks the green,
Thy certain voice we hear.
Hast thou a star to guide thy path,
Or mark the rolling year?

Delightful visitant! with thee
  I hail the time of flowers,
And hear the sound of music sweet
  From birds among the bowers.

The schoolboy, wandering through the wood
  To pull the primrose gay,
Starts, thy most curious voice to hear,
  And imitates thy lay.

What time the pea puts on the bloom,
  Thou fliest thy vocal vale,
An annual guest in other lands,
  Another Spring to hail.

Sweet bird! thy bower is ever green,
  Thy sky is ever clear;
Thou hast no sorrow in thy song,
  No Winter in thy year!

Oh, could I fly, I'd fly with thee!
  We'd make, with joyful wing,
Our annual visit o'er the globe,
  Attendants on the Spring.

THE O'LINCOLN FAMILY

By *Wilson Flagg*

A FLOCK of merry singing-birds were sport-
    ing in the grove;
  Some were warbling cheerily, and some
    were making love:

There were Bobolincon, Wadolincon, Winter-
  seeble, Conquedle, —
A livelier set was never led by tabor, pipe, or
  fiddle, —
Crying, " Phew, shew, Wadolincon, see, see, Bobo-
  lincon,
Down among the tickletops, hiding in the butter-
  cups !
I know the saucy chap, I see his shining cap
Bobbing in the clover there — see, see, see ! "

Up flies Bobolincon, perching on an apple-tree,
Startled by his rival's song, quickened by his rail-
  lery,
Soon he spies the rogue afloat, curveting in the
  air,
And merrily he turns about, and warns him to be-
  ware !
" 'Tis you that would a-wooing go, down among
  the rushes O !
But wait a week, till flowers are cheery, — wait a
  week, and ere you marry
Be sure of a house wherein to tarry !
Wadolink, Whiskodink, Tom Denny, wait, wait,
  wait ! "

Every one's a funny fellow ; every one's a little
  mellow ;
Follow, follow, follow, follow, o'er the hill and in
  the hollow !
Merrily, merrily, there they hie ; now they rise and
  now they fly ;

They cross and turn, and in and out, and down in
    the middle, and wheel about, —
With a " Phew, shew, Wadolincon! listen to me,
    Bobolincon! —
Happy's the wooing that's speedily doing, that's
    speedily doing,
That's merry and over with the bloom of the
    clover!
Bobolincon, Wadolincon, Winterseeble, follow,
    follow me!"

THE WINGED WORSHIPPERS

By *Charles Sprague*

(Addressed to two swallows that flew into the
Chauncy Place Church during divine service.)

SAY, guiltless pair,
    What seek ye from the fields of
      heaven?
      Ye have no need of prayer;
    Ye have no sins to be forgiven.

    Why perch ye here,
Where mortals to their Maker bend?
    Can your pure spirits fear
The God ye never could offend?

    Ye never knew
The crimes for which we come to weep.
    Penance is not for you,
Blessed wanderers of the upper deep.

To you 't is given
To wake sweet nature's untaught lays,
   Beneath the arch of heaven
To chirp away a life of praise.

Then spread each wing
Far, far above, o'er lakes and lands,
   And join the choirs that sing
In yon blue dome not reared with hands.

Or, if ye stay,
To note the consecrated hour,
   Teach me the airy way,
And let me try your envied power.

Above the crowd
On upward wings could I but fly,
   I'd bathe in yon bright cloud,
And seek the stars that gem the sky.

'Twere heaven indeed
Through fields of trackless light to soar,
   On nature's charms to feed,
And nature's own great God adore.

BIRCH STREAM

By Anna Boynton Averill

A T noon, within the dusty town,
      Where the wild river rushes down,
         And thunders hoarsely all day long,
I think of thee, my hermit stream,
Low singing in thy summer dream
   Thine idle, sweet, old, tranquil song.

Northward, Katahdin's chasmed pile
Looms through thy low, long, leafy aisle,
　　Eastward, Olamon's summit shines;
And I upon thy grassy shore,
The dreamful, happy child of yore,
　　Worship before mine olden shrines.

Again the sultry noontide hush
Is sweetly broken by the thrush,
　　Whose clear bell rings and dies away
Beside thy banks, in coverts deep,
Where nodding buds of orchis sleep
　　In dusk, and dream not it is day.

Again the wild cow-lily floats
Her golden-freighted, tented boats,
　　In thy cool coves of softened gloom,
O'ershadowed by the whispering reed,
And purple plumes of pickerel-weed,
　　And meadow-sweet in tangled bloom.

The startled minnows dart in flocks
Beneath thy glimmering amber rocks,
　　If but a zephyr stirs the brake;
The silent swallow swoops, a flash
Of light, and leaves, with dainty plash,
　　A ring of ripples in her wake.

—Without, the land is hot and dim;
The level fields in languor swim,
　　Their stubble-grasses brown as dust;
And all along the upland lanes,
Where shadeless noon oppressive reigns,
　　Dead roses wear their crowns of rust.

Within, is neither blight nor death,
The fierce sun wooes with ardent breath,
   But cannot win thy sylvan heart.
Only the child who loves thee long,
With faithful worship pure and strong,
   Can know how dear and sweet thou art.

So loved I thee in days gone by,
So love I yet, though leagues may lie
   Between us, and the years divide ; —
A breath of coolness, dawn, and dew, —
A joy forever fresh and true,
   Thy memory doth with me abide.

THE SONG-SPARROW

By George Parsons Lathrop

 LIMMERS gray the leafless
      thicket
    Close beside my garden gate,
Where, so light, from post to
      picket
    Hops the sparrow, blithe, se-
      date ;
Who, with meekly folded wing,
Comes to sun himself and sing.

It was there, perhaps, last year,
   That his little house he built ;
For he seems to perk and peer,
   And to twitter, too, and tilt
     The bare branches in between,
     With a fond, familiar mien.

Once, I know, there was a nest,
　Held there by the sideward thrust
Of those twigs that touch his breast ;
　　Though 'tis gone now.　Some rude gust
　　　Caught it, over-full of snow, —
　　　Bent the bush, — and stole it so.

Thus our highest holds are lost,
　By the ruthless winter's wind,
When, with swift-dismantling frost,
　　The green woods we dwelt in, thinn'd
　　　Of their leafage, grow too cold,
　　　For frail hopes of summer's mold.

But if we, with spring-days mellow,
　Wake to woeful wrecks of change,
And the sparrow's ritornello
　　Scaling still its old sweet range ;
　　　Can we do a better thing
　　　Than, with him, still build and sing?

Oh, my sparrow, thou dost breed
　Thought in me beyond all telling ;
Shootest through me sunlight, seed,
　　And fruitful blessing, with that welling
　　　Ripple of ecstatic rest
　　　Gurgling ever from thy breast !

And thy breezy carol spurs
　Vital motion in my blood,
Such as in the sap-wood stirs,
　　Swells and shapes the pointed bud
　　　Of the lilac ; and besets
　　　The hollow thick with violets.

Yet I know not any charm
  That can make the fleeting time
Of thy sylvan, faint alarm
  Suit itself to human rhyme:
    And my yearning rhythmic word
    Does thee grievous wrong, blithe bird.

So, however thou hast wrought
  This wild joy on heart and brain,
It is better left untaught.
  Take thou up the song again:
    There is nothing sad afloat
    On the tide that swells thy throat!

THE HERALD CRANE

By Hamlin Garland

AH! say you so, bold sailor
  In the sun-lit deeps of sky!
Dost thou so soon the seed-time
    tell
  In thy imperial cry,
As circling in yon shoreless sea
  Thine unseen form goes drift-
    ing by?

I can not trace in the noon-day glare
  Thy regal flight, O crane!
From the leaping might of the fiery light
  Mine eyes recoil in pain,
But on mine ear, thine echoing cry
  Falls like a bugle strain.

The mellow soil glows beneath my feet,
   Where lies the buried grain ;
The warm light floods the length and breadth,
   Of the vast, dim, shimmering plain,
Throbbing with heat and the nameless thrill
   Of the birth-time's restless pain.

On weary wing, plebeian geese
   Push on their arrowy line
Straight into the north, or snowy brant
   In dazzling sunshine, gloom and shine ;
But thou, O crane, save for thy sovereign cry,
   At thy majestic height
On proud, extended wings sweep'st on
   In lonely, easeful flight.

Then cry, thou martial-throated herald !
   Cry to the sun, and sweep
And swing along thy mateless, tireless course
   Above the clouds that sleep
Afloat on lazy air — cry on ! Send down
   Thy trumpet note — it seems
The voice of hope and dauntless will,
   And breaks the spell of dreams.

LINE UP, BRAVE BOYS

By Hamlin Garland

THE packs are on, the cinches tight,
   The patient horses wait,
   Upon the grass the frost lies white,
The dawn is gray and late.

The leader's cry rings sharp and clear,
The campfires smoulder low ;
Before us lies a shallow mere,
Beyond, the mountain snow.
> *" Line up, Billy, line up, boys,*
> *The east is gray with coming day,*
> *We must away, we cannot stay.*
> *Hy-o, hy-ak, brave boys ! "*

Five hundred miles behind us lie,
As many more ahead,
Through mud and mire on mountains high
Our weary feet must tread.
So one by one, with loyal mind,
The horses swing to place,
The strong in lead, the weak behind,
In patient plodding grace.
> *" Hy-o, Buckskin, brave boy, Joe !*
> *The sun is high,*
> *The hid loons cry :*
> *Hy-ak — away !   Hy-o ! "*

THE WHISTLING MARMOT

By Hamlin Garland

ON mountains cold and bold and high,
Where only golden eagles fly,
He builds his home against the sky.

Above the clouds he sits and whines,
The morning sun about him shines ;
Rivers loop below in shining lines.

No wolf or cat may find him there,
That winged corsair of the air,
The eagle, is his only care.

He sees the pink snows slide away,
He sees his little ones at play,
And peace fills out each summer day.

In winter, safe within his nest,
He eats his winter store with zest,
And takes his young ones to his breast.

THE TOIL OF THE TRAIL

By *Hamlin Garland*

WHAT have I gained by the toil of
the trail?
I know and know well.
I have found once again the lore
I had lost
In the loud city's hell.

I have broadened my hand to the cinch and the axe,
I have laid my flesh to the rain;
I was hunter and trailer and guide;
I have touched the most primitive wildness again.

I have threaded the wild with the stealth of the deer,
No eagle is freer than I;
No mountain can thwart me, no torrent appall,
I defy the stern sky.
So long as I live these joys will remain,
I have touched the most primitive wildness again.

PEACE

By Charles De Kay

KEEN gleams the wind, and all the
    ground
  Is bare and chapped with bitter
    cold.
The ruts are iron ; fish are found
  Encased in ice as in a mold;
The frozen hilltops ache with pain
And shudders tremble down each shy
Deep rootlet burrowing in the plain ; —
    Now mark the sky.

Softly she pulls a downy veil
  Before her clear Medusa face ;
This, falling slow, abroad doth trail
  Across the wold a feathery trace,
Whereunder soon the moaning earth
  Aslumber stretches dreamily,
Forgot both pain and summer's mirth,
    Soothed by the sky.

APRIL

By Samuel Longfellow

AGAIN has come the Spring-time,
  With the crocus's golden bloom,
With the smell of the fresh-turned earth-
    mould,
And the violet's perfume.

O gardener! tell me the secret
  Of thy flowers so rare and sweet! —
— " I have only enriched my garden
  With the black mire from the street."

NOVEMBER

By Samuel Longfellow

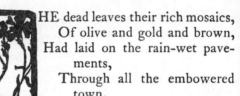

T HE dead leaves their rich mosaics,
    Of olive and gold and brown,
  Had laid on the rain-wet pave-
      ments,
    Through all the embowered
      town.

  They were washed by the au-
      tumn tempest,
They were trod by hurrying feet,
  And the maids came out with their besoms,
And swept them into the street,

To be crushed and lost forever
  'Neath the wheels, in the black mire lost, —
The Summer's precious darlings,
  She nurtured at such cost!

O words that have fallen from me!
  O golden thoughts and true!
Must I see in the leaves a symbol
  Of the fate which awaiteth you?

THE CRICKETS

By Harriet McEwen Kimball

PIPE, little minstrels of the waning
    year,
  In gentle concert pipe!
Pipe the warm noons; the mel-
    low harvest near;
  The apples dropping ripe;

The tempered sunshine and the
    softened shade;
  The trill of lonely bird;
The sweet sad hush on Nature's gladness laid;
  The sounds through silence heard!

Pipe tenderly the passing of the year;
  The Summer's brief reprieve;
The dry husk rustling round the yellow ear;
  The chill of morn and eve!

Pipe the untroubled trouble of the year;
  Pipe low the painless pain;
Pipe your unceasing melancholy cheer;
  The year is in the wane.

COME FOR ARBUTUS

By Mrs. Sara L. Oberholtzer

COME for arbutus, my dear, my dear:
  The pink waxen blossoms are waking, I hear;
  We'll gather an armful of fragrant wild cheer.
Come for arbutus, my dear, my dear,
  Come for arbutus, my dear.

Come for arbutus, my dear, my dear ;
Come through the gray meadow, and pass the
  black weir,
To brown-margined forest, and part the leaves
  sere.
Come for arbutus, my dear, my dear,
   Come for arbutus, my dear.

Come for arbutus, my dear, my dear ;
We'll gather the first virgin bloom of the year,
The blush of spring kisses with coral lips near.
Come for arbutus, my dear, my dear,
   Come for arbutus, my dear.

THE DANDELIONS

By Helen Gray Cone

UPON a showery night and still,
  Without a sound of warning,
A trooper band surprised the
  hill,
  And held it in the morning.
We were not waked by bugle-
  notes,
 No cheer our dreams invaded,
And yet, at dawn, their yellow coats
 On the green slopes paraded.

We careless folk the deed forgot ;
 Till one day, idly walking,
We marked upon the self-same spot
 A crowd of veterans talking.

They shook their trembling heads and gray
   With pride and noiseless laughter;
When, well-a-day ! they blew away,
   And ne'er were heard of after !

HYMN TO DARKNESS

By J. Norris

HAIL thou most sacred venerable
      thing !
   What Muse is worthy thee to
      sing ?
Thee, from whose pregnant uni-
      versal womb
All things, even Light thy rival,
      first did come.
What dares he not attempt that sings of thee
   Thou first and greatest mystery ?
Who can the secrets of thy essence tell ?
Thou like the light of God art inaccessible.

Before great Love this monument did raise,
   This ample theatre of praise.
Before the folding circles of the sky
Were tun'd by Him who is all harmony.
Before the morning stars their hymn began,
   Before the councel held for man.
Before the birth of either Time or Place,
Thou reign'st unquestion'd monarch in the empty
     space.

Thy native lot thou didst to Light resign,
   But still half of the globe is thine.
Here with a quiet, and yet aweful hand,
Like the best emperours thou dost command.
To thee the stars above their brightness owe,
   And mortals their repose below.
To thy protection Fear and Sorrow flee,
And those that weary are of light, find rest in thee.

Tho' light and glory be th' Almighty's throne,
   Darkness is His pavilion.
From that His radiant beauty, but from thee
He has His terror and His majesty.
Thus when He first proclaim'd His sacred Law,
   And would His rebel subjects awe,
Like princes on some great solemnity,
H' appear'd in's robes of State, and clad Himself
    with thee.
The blest above do thy sweet umbrage* prize,
   When cloy'd with light, they veil their eyes.
The vision of the Deity is made
More sweet and beatifick by thy shade.
But we poor tenants of this orb below
   Don't here thy excellencies know,
Till Death our understandings does improve,
And then our wiser ghosts thy silent night-walks love.

But thee I now admire, thee would I chuse
   For my religion, or my Muse.
'Tis hard to tell whether thy reverend shade
Has more good votaries or poets made,

        * Shadow.

From thy dark caves were inspirations given,
  And from thick groves went vows to Heaven.
Hail then thou Muse's and Devotion's spring,
'Tis just we should adore, 'tis just we should thee
    sing.

THE OVEN-BIRD

By Frank Bolles

I N the hollows of the mountains,
  In the valleys spreading from
      them,
  Stand the rustling broad-leaved
      forests,
  Trees whose leaves are shed in
      autumn.

Underneath them lie the leaf beds,
Resting one upon another,
Laid there yearly by the storm winds;
Pressed and smoothed by winter snow-drifts.

In the days of spring migrations,
Days when warbler hosts move northward,
To the forests, to the leaf beds,
Comes the tiny oven builder.

Daintily the leaves he tiptoes;
Underneath them builds his oven,
Arched and framed with last year's oak leaves,
Roofed and walled against the raindrops.

Hour by hour his voice he raises,
Mingling with the red-eye's snatches,
Answering to the hermit's anthem;
Rising — falling, like a wind breath.

Strange, ventriloquous his music,
Far away when close beside one;
Near at hand when seeming distant;
Weird — his plaintive accrescendo.

Teach us! teach us! is his asking,
Uttered to the Omnipresent:
Teach us! teach us! comes responsive
From the solemn listening forest.

When the whip-poor-will is clucking,
When the bats unfurl their canvas,
When dim twilight rules the forest,
Soaring towards the high star's radiance
Far above the highest treetop,
Singing goes this sweet Accentor.

Noontide never sees this soaring,
Midday never hears this music,
Only at the hour of slumber,
Only once, as day is dying,
When the perils and the sorrows,
When the blessings and the raptures,
One and all have joined the finished,
Does this sweet-toned forest singer
Urge his wings towards endless ether,
Hover high a single moment
Pouring out his spirit's gladness
Toward the Source of life and being.

THE SNOW-FILLED NEST

By Rose Terry Cooke

T swings upon the leafless tree,
By stormy winds blown to and
fro;
Deserted, lonely, sad to see.
　And full of cruel snow.

In　summer's　noon　the　leaves
above
Made dewy shelter from the heat;
The nest was full of life and love; —
　Ah, life and love are sweet!

The tender brooding of the day,
The silent, peaceful dreams of night,
The joys that patience overpay,
　The cry of young delight,

The song that through the branches rings,
The nestling crowd with eager eyes,
The flutter soft of untried wings,
　The flight of glad surprise : —

All, all are gone! I know not where;
And still upon the cold gray tree,
Lonely, and tossed by every air,
　That snow-filled nest I see.

I, too, had once a place of rest,
Where life, and love, and peace were mine —
Even as the wild-birds build their nest,
　When skies and summer shine.

But winter came, the leaves were dead;
The mother-bird was first to go,
The nestlings from my sight have fled;
The nest is full of snow.

THE WISTFUL DAYS

By Robert Underwood Johnson

HAT is there wanting in the
Spring?
Soft is the air as yester-
year;
The happy-nested green is
here,
And half the world is on the
wing.
The morning beckons, and like balm
Are westward waters blue and calm.
Yet something's wanting in the Spring.

What is it wanting in the Spring?
O April, lover to us all,
What is so poignant in thy thrall
When children's merry voices ring?
What haunts us in the cooing dove
More subtle than the speech of Love,
What nameless lack or loss of Spring?

Let Youth go dally with the Spring,
Call her the dear, the fair, the young;
And all her graces ever sung

Let him, once more rehearsing, sing.
 They know, who keep a broken tryst,
 Till something from the Spring be missed
We have not truly known the Spring.

TO THE HOUSATONIC AT STOCKBRIDGE

By Robert Underwood Johnson

ONTENTED river! in thy
 dreamy realm —
The cloudy willow and the
 plumy elm :
They call thee English, thinking
 thus to mate
Their musing streams that, oft
 with pause sedate,
Linger through misty meadows for a glance
At haunted tower or turret of romance.
Beware their praise who rashly would deny
To our New World its true tranquillity.
Our "New World"? Nay, say rather to our Old
(Let truth and freedom make us doubly bold);
Tell them : A thousand silent years before
Their sea born isle — at every virgin shore
Dripping like Aphrodite's tresses — rose,
Here, 'neath her purple veil, deep slept Repose,
To be awakened but by wail of war.
About thy cradle under yonder hill,
Before thou knewest bridge, or dam, or mill,
Soft winds of starlight whispered heavenly lore,

Which, like our childhood's, all the workday toil
Cannot efface, nor long its beauty soil.
Thou hast grown human laboring with men
At wheel and spindle; sorrow thou dost ken;
Yet dost thou still the unshaken stars behold,
Calm to their calm returning, as of old.
Thus, like a gentle nature that grows strong
In meditation for the strife with wrong,
Thou show'st the peace that only tumult can;
Surely, serener river never ran.

Thou beautiful! From every dreamy hill
What eye but wanders with thee at thy will,
Imagining thy silver course unseen
Convoyed by two attendant streams of green
In bending lines, — like half-expected swerves
Of swaying music, or those perfect curves
We call the robin; making harmony
With many a new-found treasure of the eye:
With meadows, marging smoothly rounded hills
Where Nature teemingly the myth fulfils
Of many-breasted Plenty; with the blue,
That to the zenith fades through triple hue,
Pledge of the constant day; with clouds of white,
That haunt horizons with their blooms of light,
And when the east with rosy eve is glowing
Seem like full cheeks of zephyrs gently blowing.

Contented river! and yet over-shy
To mask thy beauty from the eager eye;
Hast thou a thought to hide from field and town?
In some deep current of the sunlit brown

Art thou disquieted — still uncontent
With praise from thy Homeric bard, who lent
The world the placidness thou gavest him ?
Thee Bryant loved when life was at its brim ;
And when the wine was falling, in thy wood
Of sturdy willows like a Druid stood.
Oh, for his touch on this o'er-throbbing time,
His hand upon the hectic brow of Rhyme,
Cooling its fevered passion to a pace
To lead, to stir, to re-inspire the race !

.   .   .   .

Ah ! there's a restive ripple, and the swift
Red leaves — September's firstlings — faster drift ;
Betwixt twin aisles of prayer they seem to pass
(One green, one greenly mirrored in thy glass).
Wouldst thou away, dear stream ?   Come, whisper
    near !
I also of much resting have a fear :
Let me to-morrow thy companion be
By fall and shallow to the adventurous sea !

LITTLE BROTHERS OF THE GROUND

By Edwin Markham

L ITTLE ants in leafy wood,
    Bound by gentle Brotherhood,
    While ye gaily gather spoil,
Men are ground by the wheel of toil ;

While ye follow Blessed Fates,
Men are shriveled up with hates;
Or they lie with sheeted Lust,
And they eat the bitter dust.

Ye are fraters in your hall,
Gay and chainless, great and small;
All are toilers in the field,
All are sharers in the yield.
But we mortals plot and plan
How to grind the fellow-man;
Glad to find him in a pit,
If we get some gain of it.
So with us, the sons of Time,
Labor is a kind of crime,
For the toilers have the least,
While the idlers lord the feast.
Yes, our workers they are bound,
Pallid captives to the ground;
Jeered by traitors, fooled by knaves,
Till they stumble into graves.

How appears to tiny eyes
All this wisdom of the wise?

THE FLYING MIST

By Edwin Markham

I WATCH afar the moving Mystery,
The wool-shod, formless terror of the sea —
The Mystery whose lightest touch can change
The world God made to phantasy, death-strange.

Under its spell all things grow old and gray
As they will be beyond the Judgment Day.
All voices, at the lifting of some hand,
Seem calling to us from another land.
Is it the still Power of the Sepulchre
That makes all things the wraiths of things that
    were ?

It touches, one by one, the wayside posts,
And they are gone, a line of hurrying ghosts.
It creeps upon the towns with stealthy feet,
And men are phantoms on a phantom street.
It strikes the towers and they are shafts of air,
Above the spectres passing in the square.
The city turns to ashes, spire by spire ;
The mountains perish with their peaks afire.
The fading city and the falling sky
Are swallowed in one doom without a cry.

It tracks the traveller fleeing with the gale,
Fleeing toward home and friends without avail ;
It springs upon him and he is a ghost,
A blurred shape moving on a soundless coast.
God ! it pursues my love along the stream,
Swirls round her and she is forever dream.
What Hate has touched the universe with eld,
And left me only in a world dispelled ?

A STRIP OF BLUE

By Lucy Larcom

I DO not own an inch of land,
　But all I see is mine, —
The orchard and the mowing-
　　fields,
　The lawns and gardens fine.
The winds my tax-collectors
　　are,
　They bring me tithes divine, —
Wild scents and subtle essences,
　A tribute rare and free;
And, more magnificent than all,
　My window keeps for me
A glimpse of blue immensity, —
　A little strip of sea.

Richer am I than he who owns
　Great fleets and argosies;
I have a share in every ship
　Won by the inland breeze
To loiter on yon airy road
　Above the apple-trees.
I freight them with my untold dreams;
　Each bears my own picked crew;
And nobler cargoes wait for them
　Than ever India knew, —
My ships that sail into the East
　Across that outlet blue.

Sometimes they seem like living shapes, —
   The people of the sky, —
Guests in white raiment coming down
   From Heaven, which is close by;
I call them by familiar names,
   As one by one draws nigh,
So white, so light, so spirit-like,
   From violet mists they bloom!
The aching wastes of the unknown
   Are half reclaimed from gloom,
Since on life's hospitable sea
   All souls find sailing-room.

The ocean grows a weariness
   With nothing else in sight;
Its east and west, its north and south,
   Spread out from morn till night;
We miss the warm, caressing shore,
   Its brooding shade and light.
A part is greater than the whole;
   By hints are mysteries told.
The fringes of eternity, —
   God's sweeping garment-fold,
In that bright shred of glittering sea,
   I reach out for, and hold.

The sails, like flakes of roseate pearl,
   Float in upon the mist;
The waves are broken precious stones, —
   Sapphire and amethyst,
Washed from celestial basement walls
   By suns unsetting kissed.

Out through the utmost gates of space,
   Past where the gray stars drift,
To the widening Infinite, my soul
   Glides on, a vessel swift;
Yet loses not her anchorage
   In yonder azure rift.

Here sit I, as a little child:
   The threshold of God's door
Is that clear band of chrysoprase;
   Now the vast temple floor,
The blinding glory of the dome
   I bow my head before:
Thy universe, O God, is home,
   In height or depth, to me;
Yet here upon thy footstool green
   Content am I to be;
Glad, when is opened unto my need
   Some sea-like glimpse of thee.

ALBATROSS

By Charles Warren Stoddard

TIME cannot age thy sinews, nor
   the gale
Batter the network of thy feath-
   ered mail,
   Lone sentry of the deep!
Among the crashing caverns of
   the storm,
With wing unfettered, lo! thy frigid form
   Is whirled in dreamless sleep!

Where shall thy wing find rest for all its might?
Where shall thy lidless eye, that scours the night,
  Grow blank in utter death?
When shall thy thousand years have stripped thee
    bare,
Invulnerable spirit of the air,
  And sealed thy giant-breath?

Not till thy bosom hugs the icy wave, —
Not till thy palsied limbs sink in that grave,
  Caught by the shrieking blast,
And hurled upon the sea with broad wings locked,
On an eternity of waters rocked,
  Defiant to the last!

TO THE MOCKING-BIRD

By Richard Henry Wilde

INGED mimic of the woods!
    thou motley fool!
  Who shall thy gay buffoonery
      describe?
  Thine ever-ready notes of ridi-
    cule
  Pursue thy fellows still with jest
      and gibe.
Wit, sophist, songster, Yorick of thy tribe,
Thou sportive satirist of Nature's school,
To thee the palm of scoffing we ascribe,
Arch-mocker and mad Abbot of Misrule!

For such thou art by day, — but all night long
Thou pourest a soft, sweet, pensive, solemn strain,
As if thou didst in this thy moonlight song
Like to the melancholy Jacques complain,
Musing on falsehood, folly, vice, and wrong,
And sighing for thy motley coat again.

A CHRYSALIS

By *Mary Emily Bradley*

MY little Mädchen found one day
A curious something in her play,
That was not fruit, nor flower, nor seed ;
It was not anything that grew,
Or crept, or climbed, or swam, or flew ;
Had neither legs nor wings, indeed ;
And yet she was not sure, she said,
Whether it was alive or dead.

She brought it in her tiny hand
To see if I would understand,
And wondered when I made reply,
" You've found a baby butterfly."
" A butterfly is not like this,"
With doubtful look she answered me.
So then I told her what would be
Some day within the chrysalis ;
How, slowly, in the dull brown thing
Now still as death, a spotted wing,

And then another, would unfold,
Till from the empty shell would fly
A pretty creature, by and by,
All radiant in blue and gold.

" And will it, truly ? " questioned she —
Her laughing lips and eager eyes
All in a sparkle of surprise —
" And shall your little Mädchen see ? "
" She shall ! " I said.   How could I tell
That ere the worm within its shell
Its gauzy, splendid wings had spread,
My little Mädchen would be dead ?

To-day the butterfly has flown, —
She was not here to see it fly, —
And sorrowing I wonder why
The empty shell is mine alone.
Perhaps the secret lies in this :
I too had found a chrysalis,
And Death that robbed me of delight
Was but the radiant creature's flight !

THE VOICE OF THE GRASS

By Sarah Roberts Boyle

HERE I come creeping, creeping everywhere ;
By the dusty road-side,
On the sunny hill-side,
Close by the noisy brook,
In every shady nook,
I come creeping, creeping everywhere.

Here I come creeping, smiling everywhere;
    All around the open door,
    Where sit the aged poor;
    Here where the children play,
    In the bright and merry May,
I come creeping, creeping everywhere.

Here I come creeping, creeping everywhere;
    In the noisy city street
    My pleasant face you'll meet,
    Cheering the sick at heart
    Toiling his busy part —
Silently creeping, creeping everywhere.

Here I come creeping, creeping everywhere;
    You cannot see me coming,
    Nor hear my low sweet humming;
    For in the starry night,
    And the glad morning light,
I come quietly creeping everywhere.

Here I come creeping, creeping everywhere;
    More welcome than the flowers
    In Summer's pleasant hours:
    The gentle cow is glad,
    And the merry bird not sad,
To see me creeping, creeping everywhere.

Here I come creeping, creeping everywhere:
    When you're numbered with the dead
    In your still and narrow bed,
    In the happy spring I'll come
    And deck your silent home —
Creeping, silently creeping everywhere.

Here I come creeping, creeping everywhere;
My humble song of praise
Most joyfully I raise
To Him at whose command
I beautify the land,
Creeping, silently creeping everywhere.

THE LONELY-BIRD

In the Adirondacks

By Harrison Smith Morris

DAPPLED throat of white!
Shy, hidden bird!
Perched in green dimness of
the dewy wood,
And murmuring, in that lonely,
lover mood,
Thy heart-ache, softly heard,
Sweetened by distance, over land and lake.

Why, like a kinsman, do I feel thy voice
Awaken voices in me free and sweet?
Was there some far ancestral birdhood fleet
That rose and would rejoice:
A broken cycle rounded in a song?

The lake, like steady wine in a deep cup,
Lay crystal in the curving mountain deeps;
And now the air brought that long lyric up
That sobs, then falls and weeps,
And hushes silence into listening hope.

Is it that we were sprung of one old kin,
    Children of brooding earth, that lets us tell,
      Thou from thy rhythmic throat, I deep within,
        These syllables of her spell,
This hymnèd wisdom of her pondering years ?

For thou hast spoken song-wise in a tongue
    I knew not till I heard the buried air
      Burst from the boughs and bring me what thou
        sung,
      Here where the lake lies bare
To reaching summits and the azure sky.

Thy music is a language of the trees,
    The brown soil, and the never-trodden brake ;
      Translatress art thou of dumb mysteries
        That dream through wood and lake ;
And I, in thee, have uttered what I am !

TO A CATY-DID

By Philip Freneau

N a branch of willow hid
Sings the evening Caty-did :
From the lofty locust bough
Feeding on a drop of dew,
In her suit of green arrayed
Hear her singing in the shade —
    Caty-did, Caty-did, Caty-did !

    While upon a leaf you tread,
Or repose your little head
On your sheet of shadows laid,
All the day you nothing said :

Half the night your cheery tongue
Revelled out its little song,—
   Nothing else but Caty-did.

From your lodging on the leaf
Did you utter joy or grief?
Did you only mean to say,
I have had my summer's day,
And am passing, soon, away
To the grave of Caty-did;
   Poor, unhappy Caty-did!

But you would have uttered more
Had you known of Nature's power;
From the world when you retreat,
And a leaf's your winding sheet,
Long before your spirit fled,
Who can tell but Nature said,—
Live again, my Caty-did!
   Live, and chatter Caty-did.

Tell me, what did Caty do?
Did she mean to trouble you?
Why was Caty not forbid
To trouble little Caty-did?
Wrong, indeed, at you to fling,
Hurting no one while you sing,—
   Caty-did! Caty-did! Caty-did!

Why continue to complain?
Caty tells me she again
Will not give you plague or pain;

Caty says you may be hid,
Caty will not go to bed
While you sing us Caty-did, —
    Caty-did! Caty-did! Caty-did!

But, while singing, you forgot,
To tell us what did Caty *not :*
Caty did not think of cold,
Flocks retiring to the fold,
Winter with his wrinkles old;
Winter, that yourself foretold
    When you gave us Caty-did.

Stay serenely on your nest;
Caty now will do her best,
All she can, to make you blest;
But you want no human aid, —
Nature, when she formed you, said,
    " Independent you are made,
My dear little Caty-did :
Soon yourself must disappear
With the verdure of the year,"
And to go, we know not where,
    With your song of Caty-did.

ELUSIVE NATURE

By Henry Timrod

AT last, beloved Nature! I have met
Thee face to face upon thy breezy hills,
And boldly, where thy inmost bowers are set,
Gazed on thee naked in thy mountain rills.

When first I felt thy breath upon my brow,
Tears of strange ecstasy gushed out like rain,
And with a longing, passionate as vain,
I strove to clasp thee. But, I know not how,
Always before me didst thou seem to glide;
And often from one sunny mountain-side,
Upon the next bright peak I saw thee kneel,
And heard thy voice upon the billowy blast;
But, climbing, only reached that shrine to feel
The shadow of a Presence which had passed.

THE HERMIT THRUSH

By Mrs. Nelly Hart Woodworth

WHO sings New England's Angelus?
A little bird so plainly dressed
With robe of brown and spotted vest
He rings New England's Angelus.

MIDSUMMER INVITATION

By Myron B. Benton

O PALLID student! leave thy dim alcove
And stretch one restful summer after-
noon,
Thoughtless amidst the thoughtless things of
June,
Beneath these boughs with light and murmur wove.

Drop book and pen, a thrall releasèd rove;
  The Sisyphean task flung off, impugn
  The withered Sphynx — with earth's fresh heart
    attune.
Thou, man, the origin of evil prove!
O leave that dark coil where the spider delves
  To trap the unwary reasoner in his lair,
And weave oblivon's veils round learnéd shelves;
Wist to the beat of Ariel's happy wings,
  And cool thy brain in this balm laden air;
Here brooding peace shall still thy questionings.

"THERE IS ONE SPOT FOR WHICH MY SOUL WILL YEARN"

By Myron B. Benton

THERE is one spot for which my
  soul will yearn,
  May it but come where breeze
  and sunlight play,
  And leaves are glad, some path
  of swift return;
  A waif — a presence borne on
  friendly ray —
Even thus, if but beneath the same blue sky!
The grazing kine not then will see me cross
The pasture slope; the swallows will not shy,
Nor brooding thrush; blithe bees the flowers will
  toss:

Not the faint thistle down *my* breath may charm.
Ah, me ! But I shall find the dear ways old,
If I have leave, that sheltered valley farm ;
Its climbing woods, its spring, the meadow's gold ;
 The creek-path, dearest to my boyhood's feet —
 Oh God ! is there another world so sweet ?

JOY-MONTH

By David Atwood Wasson

H, hark to the brown thrush !
  hear how he sings !
 How he pours the dear pain
  of his gladness !
What a gush ! and from out
  what golden springs !
 What a rage of how sweet
  madness !

And golden the buttercup blooms by the way,
 A song of the joyous ground ;
While the melody rained from yonder spray
 Is a blossom in fields of sound.

How glisten the eyes of the happy leaves !
 How whispers each blade, " I am blest ! "
Rosy Heaven his lips to flowered earth gives,
 With the costliest bliss of his breast.

Pour, pour of the wine of thy heart, O Nature !
 By cups of field and of sky,
By the brimming soul of every creature ! —
 Joy-mad, dear Mother, am I.

Tongues, tongues for my joy, for my joy! more
    tongues ! —
    Oh, thanks to the thrush on the tree,
To the sky, and to all earth's blooms and songs !
    They utter the heart in me.

NOVEMBER IN ENGLAND

By Thomas Hood

O sun — no moon !
No morn — no noon !
No dawn—no dusk—no prop-
    er time of day —
No sky — no earthly view —
No distance looking blue —
No road—no street—no "t'other
    side the way" —
    No end to any " Row " —
    No indications where the Crescents go —
    No top to any steeple —
No recognitions of familiar people —
    No courtesies for showing 'em —
    No knowing 'em!
No travelling at all — no locomotion,
No inkling of the way — no notion —
    "No go" — by land or ocean —
    No mail — no post —
    No news from any foreign coast —
No park — no ring — no afternoon gentility —
    No company — no nobility —

No warmth, no cheerfulness, no healthful ease,
      No comfortable feel in any member —
No shade, no shine, no butterflies, no bees,
      No fruits, no flowers, no leaves, no birds,
      November!

TO AN ALASKAN GLACIER

By *Charles Keeler*

OUT of the cloud-world sweeps
     thy awful form,
Vast frozen river, fostered by the
     storm
Up on the drear peak's snow-
     encumbered crest,
Thy sides deep grinding in the
     mountain's breast
As down its slopes thou ploughest to the sea
To leap into thy mother's arms, and be
There cradled into nothingness.   How slow,
How imperceptible, thy ceaseless flow,
As one with an eternity unspent
Wherein to round thy task of wonderment!
Thy strength resistless is as will of fate;
The granite ground to sand beneath thy weight,
The mountains hollowed out with furrows deep,
The sculptured peaks that totter from their steep,
All bear the matchless impress of thy skill,
Grim mountain hewer!   With a sudden thrill

Great bergs crash thunderously beneath the tide,
And, slow emerging, o'er the waters ride
Like boats of pearl slow floating to their doom,
Which, fondly, the soft lapping waves consume.

I walked erstwhile upon thy frozen waves,
And heard the streams amid thy ice-locked caves;
I peered down thy crevasses blue and dim,
Standing in awe upon the dizzy rim.
Beyond me lay the inlet still and blue,
Behind, the mountains loomed upon the view
Like storm-wraiths gathered from the low-hung sky.
A gust of wind swept past with heavy sigh,
And lo! I listened to the ice-stream's song
Of winter, when the nights grow dark and long,
And bright stars flash above thy fields of snow,
The cold waste sparkling in the pallid glow,
Or, when the storms wail round thy peaks and
        spires,
Playing weird notes upon thy ice-wrought lyres
Until the shuddering pinnacles, astrain,
Tumble and crash amidst the seething main.
Years, centuries and eons thou hast known,
Waxing and waning in the wilds alone,
Hoar mountain sculptor, shaper of the earth!
The crystals of the snow which gave thee birth,
Renewing still thy life, are o'er thee spread,
And, as they fall, thou quiverest in thy bed,
Stretching thy vastness down its narrow way
And roaring like a god in fierce dismay;
Thus prisoned, eager in one mighty throe
To leap into the sea and end thy woe!

SUMMER DROUGHT

By J. P. Irvine

HEN winter came the land was
  lean and sere :
 There fell no snow, and oft
  from wild and field
In famished tameness came the
  drooping deer,
 And licked the waste about
  the troughs congealed.

And though at spring we ploughed and proffered
 seed,
 It lay ungermed, a pillage for the birds :
And unto one low dam, in urgent need,
 We daily drove the suppliant, lowing herds.

But now the fields to barren waste have run,
 The dam a pool of oozing greenery lies,
Where knots of gnats hang reeling in the sun
 Till early dusk, when tilt the dragon-flies.

All night the craw-fish deepens out her wells,
 As shows the clay that freshly curbs them
  round ;
And many a random upheaved tunnel tells
 Where ran the mole across the fallow ground.

But ah ! the stone-dumb dullness of the dawn,
 When e'en the cocks too listless are to crow,
And lies the world as from all life withdrawn,
 Unheeding and outworn and swooning low !

There is no dew on any greenness shed,
  The hard-baked earth is cracked across the
    walks;
The very burrs in stunted clumps are dead
  And mullein leaves drop withered from the
    stalks.

Yet, ere the noon, as brass the heaven turns,
  The cruel sun smites with unerring aim,
The sight and touch of all things blinds and burns,
  And bare, hot hills seem shimmering into flame!

On either side the shoe-deep dusted lane
  The meagre wisps of fennel scorch to wire;
Slow lags a team that drags an empty wain,
  And, creaking dry, a wheel runs off its tire.

No flock upon the naked pasture feeds,
  The sheep with prone heads huddle near the
    fence;
A gust runs crackling through the brittle weeds,
  And then the heat still waxes more intense.

On outspread wings a hawk, far poised on high,
  Quick swooping screams, and then is heard no
    more:
The strident shrilling of a locust nigh
  Breaks forth, and dies in silence as before.

No transient cloud o'erskims with flakes of shade
  The landscape hazed in dizzy gleams of heat;
A dove's wing glances like a parried blade,
  And western walls the beams in torrents beat.

So burning low, and lower still the sun,
　In fierce white fervor, sinks anon from sight,
And so the dread, despairing day is done,
　And dumbly broods again the haggard night.

INDIAN SUMMER

By J. P. Irvine

AT last the toil encumbered days
　　are over,
　　And airs of noon are mellow
　　　as the morn ;
The blooms are brown upon the
　　seeding clover,
　　And brown the silks that
　　　plume the ripening corn.

All sounds are hushed of reaping and of mowing ;
　The winds are low ; the waters lie uncurled ;
Nor thistle-down nor gossamer is flowing,
　So lull'd in languid indolence the world.

And mute the farms along the purple valley,
　The full barns muffled to the beams with sheaves;
You hear no more the noisy rout and rally
　Amongst the tenant-masons of the eaves.

A single quail, upstarting from the stubble,
　Darts whirring past and quick alighting down
Is lost, as breaks and disappears a bubble,
　Amid the covert of the leafy brown.

The upland glades are flecked afar in dapples
  By flocks of lambs a-gambol from the fold;
The orchards bend beneath the weight of apples,
  And groves are bright in crimson and in gold.

But hark! I hear the pheasant's muffled drumming,
  The water murmur from a distant dell;
A drowsy bee in mazy tangles humming;
  The far, faint tinkling tenor of a bell.

And now from yonder beech trunk sheer and sterile,
  The rat-tat-tat of the wood-pecker's bill;
The sharp staccato barking of a squirrel,
  A dropping nut, and all again is still.

AN AUGUST AFTERNOON

On the Farm

By *J. P. Irvine*

I N stifling mows the men became oppressed,
      And hastened forth hard breathing and o'ercome;
  The hatching hen stood panting in her nest,
      The sick earth swooned in languor and was dumb.

The dust-dull'd crickets lay in heedless ease
  Of trampling hoofs along the beaten drives,
And from the fields the home-returning bees,
  Limp wing'd and tired, lit short before their hives.

The drooping dog moped aimlessly around;
  Lop'd down, got up, snapt at the gnats; in pits
Knee deep, the tethered horses stamped the ground,
  And switched at bot-flies dabbing yellow nits.

With heads held prone the sheep in huddles stood
  Through fear of gads — the lambs, too, ceased
    to romp;
The cows were wise to seek the covert wood,
  Or belly deep stand hidden in the swamp.

So dragged the day, but when the dusk grew deep
  The stagnant heat increased; we lit no light,
But sat out-doors, too faint and sick for sleep;
  Such was the stupor of that August night.

IN MAY

(1870)

By Robert Kelly Weeks

NOW that the green hill-side has
      quite
  Forgot that it was ever white,
  With quivering grasses clothed
      upon;
  And dandelions invite the sun;
  And columbines have found a
      way
To overcome the hard and gray
Old rocks that also feel the spring;
And birds make love and swing and sing,

On boughs which were so bare of late;
And bees become importunate;
And butterflies are quite at ease
Upon the well-contented breeze,
Which only is enough to make
A shadowy laughter on the lake;
And all the clouds, that here and there
Are floating, melting in the air,
Are such as beautify the blue; —
Now what is worthier, May, than you
Of all my praise, of all my love,
Except whom you remind me of?

INDEX BY AUTHORS

(The abbreviations Am. and Brit. are used respectively to indicate the American and British authors.)

339

GALLAGHER, William D. (Am.): *August,*
228 ; *The Cardinal Bird,* 230.
Garland, Hamlin (Am.): *Line Up, Brave
Boys,* 298 ; *The Herald Crane,* 297 ; *The
Toil of the Trail,* 300 ; *The Whistling Marmot,*
299.
Gilder, Richard Watson (Am.): *A Song of Early
Autumn,* 223 ; *Dawn,* 220; " *Great Nature is
an Army Gay,*" 224 ; *The Voice of the Pine,*
221.

HARTE, Francis Bret (Am.): *Grizzly,*
197 ; *To a Sea-Bird,* 196.
Herrick, Robert (Brit.): *To Blossoms,* 11.
Heywood, Thomas (Brit.): *Pack Clouds
Away,* 10.
Hill, Thomas (Am.): *The Bobolink,* 153.
Hogg, James (Brit.): *The Lark,* 280.
Holmes, Oliver Wendell (Am.): *Midsummer,* 106 ;
My Aviary, 102 ; *To an Insect,* 107.
Hood, Thomas (Brit.): *November in England,*
330.
Howells, William Dean (Am.): *The Song the Oriole
Sings,* 74.
Howitt, Mary (Brit.): *Cornfields,* 206.

IRVINE, J. P. (Am.): *An August Afternoon,*
336; *Indian Summer,* 335 ; *Summer Drought,*
333.

* Common Pilewort.

BIRD POEMS

FLOWER POEMS

POEMS OF NATURE

SPRING

AUTUMN

WINTER

GENERAL NATURE

357